The Women's Cookbook

The Women's

by Lis Bensley

Cookbook

and Colleen Sullivan

VIKING

VIKING
Viking Penguin Inc., 40 West 23rd Street,
New York, New York 10010, U.S.A.
Penguin Books Ltd, Harmondsworth,
Middlesex, England
Penguin Books Australia Ltd, Ringwood,
Victoria, Australia
Penguin Books Canada Limited, 2801 John Street,
Markham, Ontario, Canada L3R 1B4
Penguin Books (N.Z.) Ltd, 182–190 Wairau Road,
Auckland 10, New Zealand

First published in 1986 by Viking Penguin Inc.
Published simultaneously in Canada

LIBRARY OF CONGRESS CATALOGING IN PUBLICATION DATA
Bensley, Lis.
    The women's cookbook.
    Includes index.
    1. Diet therapy.   2. Women—Diseases—Diet therapy.
3. Women—Nutrition.   4. Cookery for the sick.
I. Sullivan, Colleen.   II. Title.
RM217.B46   1986   613.2′088042   85-40995
ISBN 0-670-80738-9

Third printing April 1987

Printed in the United States of America by
R. R. Donnelley & Sons Company, Harrisonburg, Virginia
Set in Video Garamond
Design by Ann Gold

The Women's

by Lis Bensley

The Women's Cookbook

Contents

Introduction

We first decided to join forces and develop a very special nutrition guide and cookbook for women when we worked together on an earlier book, *PMS/Premenstrual Syndrome.* It was during the research for that book that the issue of preventing and correcting health problems through diet came up. It fascinated both of us.

Lis Bensley, who had studied at Paris's Cordon Bleu School of Cooking and who has always had a strong interest in sound nutrition, developed the recipes. Our aim was to create tasty gourmet meals with maximum nutritional benefits and to include recipes that would be easy to prepare at the end of a busy workday. Although we have called this book *The Women's Cookbook,* these recipes are suitable for anyone who wants to keep off the high-calorie circuit and who is interested in getting the most nutritional value out of his or her food. My role was to continue the research into nutrition and health that began with the *PMS* book and to organize the text portion, providing the guidelines on which Lis based her recipes. We believe that there is no single source of health/dietary information for women—despite the new attention to health problems specific to women—and hope that our text fills that gap.

—COLLEEN SULLIVAN
November 1985

The Women's Cookbook

One

Good Taste, Good Health

*F*ine cuisine is one of the priorities of the affluent American lifestyle. But we are no longer willing to sit before dishes buried in butter and cream or swimming in salty sauces. What can we do if we want the taste, the creativity, the elegance of gourmet meals without the calories, the salt, and the fats? And how can anyone with a busy schedule—with career, family, and community demands—find the time to do anything about dinner but eat Chinese takeout or pop processed foods into the microwave?

Those were the dilemmas that we discussed before deciding to write this cookbook. For we knew what people around the country are just beginning to realize: it is possible to combine good taste with good health to produce easy-to-prepare gourmet meals.

More and more, that message is being heard. But for those who can't afford the luxurious "light" meals of New York's elegant Four Seasons or the nouvelle entrées of the three-star Parisian establishment Archestrate, we have developed a recipe plan that requires a minimum of preparation time and average cooking skills. To heighten their nutritional value, the recipes emphasize fresh foods: the best vegetables, fruits, meats, a range of herbs, seasonings, and whole grains. The result is something that women have needed for years: a gourmet cookbook that increases nutrition, not calories, that emphasizes both flavor and health.

We have introduced our recipe and menu section with a complete guide to women's concerns about diet. Read on, and you'll learn how to modify your eating habits to prevent heart disease and cancer, how to ease the symptoms of premenstrual syndrome through diet, why too much protein adds weight and can lead to osteoporosis, and much, much more.

Before going further, let's take a look at the basic substances that are the brick and mortar of this factory, the human body, and at how those substances work.

CARBOHYDRATES

Carbohydrates are essential substances in forming the body's cells. There are two kinds of carbohydrates: complex carbohydrates, which are starches, including whole grains, legumes, fruits, and vegetables; and simple carbohydrates, or sugars, including glucose and fructose.

In later chapters you'll learn how important—and how ignored—carbohydrates are in our diets.

FATS

Fat is one of those substances that the body has in abundance and that we keep adding to—in excess amounts every day. The body makes fat from proteins and carbohydrates in the diet if the diet contains more calories than are needed for energy on a daily basis. That's how we get fat. Body fat is a warehouse for calories; your body uses the stored calories when it needs more energy than your diet supplies. That's why people lose body fat on a low-calorie diet.

To shed 1 pound of excess fat, your diet must build up an energy deficit of 3,500 calories. That's why it takes so long to achieve a real and lasting weight loss.

The average adult only needs 1 tablespoon of fat to maintain good nutrition. Yet the typical American eats 6 to 8 tablespoons of fat a day. Even if you pass up butter and margarine and mayonnaise and salad dressings, there is hidden fat in your food—in meats, dairy products, nuts, even fruits and vegetables.

What is this troublesome substance anyway? Deposits of body fat help to support and cushion vital organs, protecting them from injury. Since fat is a poor conductor of heat, the layer of fat under your skin provides insulation against extremes of heat and cold. Fat deposits in muscles are a source of energy for the muscles, including the heart. (Fats provide 9 calories per gram of energy, more than twice the level provided by carbohydrates and proteins.) Fatty oils in the skin and hair prevent dryness and give your complexion a healthy glow. Fats are also the construction material for hormone-like regulatory substances called prostaglandins. Without some body fat, women's sex-hormone balance and menstrual cycle are disrupted. This happens when the percentage of body fat falls to a level too low to support the development of a fetus.

Fat also helps the body absorb some essential nutrients. Vitamins A, E, D, and K are fat-soluble vitamins, transported in fat and broken down in fat. To absorb vitamins, about 10 percent of your total caloric intake needs to be fat. You can get that much simply from eating fish and vegetables, however.

There are different kinds of fats, of course.

Saturated fats are in meat, butter, dairy products, and oils. They raise the cholesterol level and are not needed in our diet at all. Unsaturated fats, such as olive and peanut oils, don't raise or lower cholesterol levels. Polyunsaturated fats, found in corn, safflower, and soybean oils, actually lower cholesterol. Fish is high in polyunsaturated fats.

PROTEIN

Protein is the essential building block of the cell. Every cell in your body contains some protein. Excluding water, 50 percent of the body's weight is protein; it is part of muscle, bone, cartilage, skin, blood, and the lymph system. All enzymes and many hormones are proteins. The protein of muscle is also the tissue that contracts and holds water; the protein in hair, skin, and nails is hard and insoluble, providing a protective coating for the body. The protein in blood vessels is elastic, allowing them to expand and contract, to maintain normal blood pressure. Protein is also part of the rigid framework of bones and teeth.

With protein, the body forms new tissues, replaces worn-out ones, regulates the balance of water and acids, and transports nutrients in and out of cells. Protein is needed to make antibodies, it transports oxygen and nutrients in the blood, and it is essential to the clotting of blood and the formation of scar tissue.

Living tissue contains twenty-two different kinds of amino acids, or proteins. The body has no storage organ for protein; protein needs to be supplied daily. After only one day without protein the body starts breaking down protein in nonessential tissue like muscle to support the vital organs. That's why you need a daily intake of complete protein.

While animal proteins—meat, fish, poultry, dairy products, and eggs—are complete proteins, vegetable proteins are incomplete. When vegetable proteins are eaten in conjunction with other vegetables or fish, however, complete proteins can be built. Rice, for example, is an incomplete protein. But eaten with legumes, wheat, or sesame seeds, it becomes complete, as do legumes eaten with corn, rice, wheat, sesame seeds, barley, or oats.

Slightly more than a 2-ounce portion of most meats, chicken, and fish fulfills about one-third of an adult woman's daily protein needs. The daily recommended dietary allowance for protein for adults nineteen and over, in terms of per pound of ideal body weight, is 0.36 grams; pregnant women need 0.62 grams, and nursing women 0.53 grams. (Multiply your ideal body weight times 0.36 grams: for example, a 120-pound woman would require 43.2 grams of protein a day.)

However, most Americans consume many more times their essential protein requirement each day. In fact, despite the popularity of high-protein, low-carbohydrate diets, this overconsumption of protein is one of the contributing factors to our overweight society. An excess of protein is of no use to the body except as an energy source—that is, calories. And calories not burned up each day are stored as fat. The most common sources of protein—meats and cheese—are high in fat and calories. Most contain a greater percentage of calories from fat than from protein. That excess puts a strain on the liver and kidneys, which have to process the protein so it can be excreted. (People with kidney diseases are automatically put on low-protein diets.) Excess protein promotes bone loss and the fractures that result, because it causes the body to lose calcium (in the liver-kidney excretion process) and increases body fat. For women, this is a dangerous situation that leads to osteoporosis.

Most people aren't aware of the amount of protein in their food, or of the abundance of protein available from non-meat and dairy sources. The following table provides the evidence.

PROTEIN IN FOOD

Food	Portion	Protein (*in grams*)
Bacon	2 medium slices	3.8
Beef, chuck roast	3 oz.	24.0
Beef, lean ground (raw)	¼ lb.	23.4
Bologna	3 slices (3 oz.)	10.2
Cheese, American	1-oz. slice	6.6
Cheese, Cheddar	1 oz.	7.1
Cheese, cottage	½ cup	15.0
Chicken, fried	1 drumstick	12.2
Eggs	2 medium	11.4
Fish sticks	3	14.1
Flounder	3 oz.	25.5
Frankfurter	1	7.1
Ham, boiled	3 slices (3 oz.)	16.2
Lamb, rib chop	3 oz.	17.9
Liver, chicken	1	6.6
Mackerel	3 oz.	18.6
Milk, skim	1 cup	8.8
Peanut butter	2 tbsp.	8.0
Pizza, cheese	¼ (14-in.) pie	15.6
Pork, loin	3 oz.	20.8
Pork sausage	2 links	5.4
Scallops, fried	3 oz.	16.0
Shrimp, fried	3 oz.	11.6
Tuna, canned	3 oz. drained	24.4
Turkey	3 oz.	26.8
Yogurt	1 cup	8.3
Banana	1 medium	1.3
Barley	¼ cup, raw	4.1
Bean curd (tofu)	1 piece	9.4
Beans, kidney	½ cup, cooked	7.2
Beans, lima	½ cup, cooked	6.5
Beans, navy	½ cup, cooked	7.4

Food	Portion	Protein (*in grams*)
Bean sprouts	½ cup	2.0
Bran Flakes (40%)	1 cup	3.6
Bread, rye	1 slice	2.3
Bread, white	1 slice	2.4
Bread, whole wheat	1 slice	2.6
Broccoli	½ cup	2.4
Bulgur	1 cup, cooked	8.4
Corn	½ cup kernels	2.7
Farina	1 cup, cooked in water	3.2
Lentils	½ cup, cooked	7.8
Macaroni	1 cup, cooked	6.5
Muffin, corn	1 medium	2.8
Noodles, egg	1 cup, cooked	6.6
Oatmeal	1 cup, cooked in water	4.8
Pancakes	3 (4-in.) cakes	5.7
Peas, green	½ cup, cooked	4.3
Potato, baked	7 oz.	4.0
Rice, brown	1 cup, cooked	4.9
Rice, white	1 cup, cooked	4.1
Sesame seeds	1 tbsp.	1.5
Spaghetti	1 cup, cooked	6.5
Squash, acorn, baked	1 cup	3.9
Sweet potato, baked	5 oz.	2.4
Walnuts	10 large	7.3
Wheat, shredded	2 biscuits	5.0

Weight control is a daily, lifelong project for many women, especially those who have a genetic or behavioral tendency to put on weight. But it doesn't have to be a goal accomplished by denial; the purpose of this book is to show you how to develop a nutrition and diet program that is enjoyable, tasty, and easy to prepare.

Underscoring the urgency of the pounds-per-inch pressure are some worrisome facts. Obesity kills, and it doesn't take too many pounds to put you in the "obesity" category. That was the message sent by a fourteen-member panel of nutritionists and physicians assembled in early 1985 by the National Institutes of Health. After reviewing a wealth of research data, the panel concluded that being overweight by just 20 percent or more of one's ideal body weight presents "a very pervasive health hazard in many systems of the body." The 20-percent measurement means that 34 million American adults, or about 1 out of 5 people over the age of nineteen, are considered to be obese. Of these, 11 million are "severely obese," exceeding their desirable weights by 40 percent or more. Obese persons have three times the normal incidence of high blood pressure and diabetes, an increased risk of heart disease, a shorter lifespan, and an unusually high risk of developing certain types of cancer, respiratory disorders, and arthritis.

Overweight women have five times the normal risk of developing cancer of the uterine lining and a higher risk of breast and cervical cancers. Even the distribution of fat on the body seems to influence health, researchers say. Studies show that people who carry their excess fat around their midsection as a "spare tire" are more apt to suffer heart disease, stroke, and diabetes than those who carry the same amount of excess pounds around their hips and thighs. No evidence as to why this is true has been uncovered yet. It would seem easy to scare oneself into dieting.

DESIRABLE WEIGHT FOR WOMEN (by frame, ages 25-59)

Weight in Pounds (In Indoor Clothing)

HEIGHT		SMALL FRAME	MEDIUM FRAME	LARGE FRAME
Feet	*Inches*			
4	10	102–111	109–121	118–131
4	11	103–113	111–123	120–134
5	0	104–115	113–126	122–137
5	1	106–118	115–129	125–140
5	2	108–121	118–132	128–143
5	3	111–124	121–135	131–147
5	4	114–127	124–138	134–151
5	5	117–130	127–141	137–155
5	6	120–133	130–144	140–159
5	7	123–136	133–147	143–163
5	8	126–139	136–150	146–167
5	9	129–142	139–153	149–170
5	10	132–145	142–156	152–173

Copyright 1983 Metropolitan Life Insurance Company. Reprinted with permission.

Most active women of average height who do not need to lose weight should limit their daily food intake to 1,500 calories. There are many exceptions, of course. Some very active, very tall women or those with a high metabolic rate may ingest 2,000 calories a day and not gain weight; some small-boned women or those with slow metabolic rates may find they gain weight if they eat more than 1,000 calories a day. You know your body better than anyone else and undoubtedly are already aware of how much you can eat simply to maintain your weight.

Most women—of average height, frame, and metabolic rate—will lose about a pound a week on a diet limited to 1,000 calories a day. To lose faster calls for an even greater caloric restriction. But don't start any serious diet—and certainly not one of less than 1,000 calories a day—without consulting your physician first.

DIETARY GUIDELINES

How much you eat should be a factor of your need to control your weight. But *what* you eat should be a response to other concerns: avoiding such health problems as heart disease, cancer, and premenstrual syndrome. To that end, we recommend some very basic dietary guidelines.

Refined sugar is not merely packed with empty calories, providing no positive nutritional benefit, but it can also trigger metabolic reactions in the body such as depression, mood swings, crying jags, irritability, fatigue, and other side effects. It also contributes to such conditions as yeast infections. Reduce your refined sugar intake to 5 teaspoons a day. Do your best to eliminate candy, chocolate, cake, pie, pastries, and ice cream from your diet, or at least restrict them to special treats. Eat fresh fruit for dessert instead.

Salt is another substance that causes problems: it raises blood pressure and contributes to a higher rate of hypertension and heart attacks. Reduce your salt intake to less than 3 grams a day. Avoid most processed and fast foods, which contain large amounts of salt, sugar, and chemicals. Soft drinks, club soda, and tonic waters—even diet sodas—have large amounts of salt in the form of sodium benzoate. Try drinking seltzer, mineral water, or plain tap water on ice instead.

Soft drinks are no-nos for other reasons. They contain vast amounts of phosphorus, which the body doesn't need and which can cause the body to excrete the calcium that women do need. **And** except for the new caffeine-free brands, soft drinks harbor reservoirs of caffeine. Caffeine also raises blood pressure and is linked to higher risks of heart disease and cancer. Sharply reduce or eliminate your intake of caffeine (coffee, tea, soft drinks with caffeine, chocolate). Use decaffeinated coffee or tea.

Protein should account for no more than 20 percent of total daily calories. That allows for 4 ounces of protein on a 1,000-calorie diet or 7 ounces of protein on a 1,500-calorie diet.

The best sources of protein are fish, poultry, whole grains, and legumes. Red meat should be limited to 3 ounces a day.

Dairy products—eggs, cheese, milk, yogurt, butter—should be limited to 2 servings a day. Limit eggs to 3 egg yolks a week, including eggs used as ingredients in other dishes.

MEAT

Poultry—chicken, turkey, Cornish hen
Veal—especially the leg, loin and shoulder, cutlets (avoid patties; they usually include beef fat)
Fresh white fish (frozen is too salty)
Lamb—steak, leg, chop (trim all fat)
Beef—only lean cuts, such as tenderloin, rump, round steak or roast, London broil, braciole, eye of round, 90 percent lean hamburger
Pork—sometimes the loin is lean enough

In preparing meats, poultry, and fish, try to broil, bake, boil, or poach; do not fry. Remove skin from poultry; trim fat from meats. Do not use fats in cooking. If the meat you choose is marbled in fat, omit 1 serving of fat for each 1 ounce of meat you eat each day.

FISH

Almost all fresh and frozen fish are acceptable; avoid salted and pickled fish and those packed in brine or oil. Choose instead canned tuna and salmon packed in water with reduced salt. Shellfish are high in sodium but low in fat; women with problems with fluid retention may want to limit these items.

Bluefish	Scallops
Clams	Sea bass
Flounder	Shrimp
Halibut	Snapper
Lobster	Sole
Monkfish	Trout
Oysters	Tuna
Salmon	Whiting

DAIRY PRODUCTS

Limit to 2 servings a day and 3 egg yolks per week, including yolks
in cooked foods. 1 serving equals 4 ounces of skim milk, or low-fat
yogurt without sugar or fruit, or 2 ounces of evaporated skim milk
or 4 ounces of buttermilk.

FATTY FOODS

Limit fats to 20 percent or less of total calories.
1 serving contains 5 grams fat and 45 calories; the following food
amounts each equal one serving.
(All nuts and seeds should be salt-free.)

1 teaspoon butter
1 teaspoon margarine
2 tablespoons coffee cream (light)
2 tablespoons sour cream
1 tablespoon heavy cream (whipping cream)
1 tablespoon cream cheese
1 teaspoon oil (any kind, but corn oil and safflower oil are better)
2 teaspoons Miracle Whip
1 teaspoon mayonnaise
⅛ avocado
1 tablespoon almonds
2 Brazil nuts
5 filberts
1 teaspoon pecans
1½ tablespoons pine nuts or pignoli
15 pistachio nuts
1 tablespoon pumpkin seeds
2 teaspoons sesame seeds
1 tablespoon walnuts

COMPLEX CARBOHYDRATES

Complex carbohydrates should account for 50 to 65 percent of total calories—the higher the percentage the better. The following are complex carbohydrates:

VEGETABLES

One serving equals ½ cup of fresh or frozen vegetables, no salt added. Dietetic canned or no-salt vegetables may also be used. Avoid sauerkraut. Do not add salt in cooking.

Asparagus	Chard	Rhubarb
Bean sprouts	Collard greens	Rutabaga
Beet greens	Dandelion greens	Spinach
Beets	Eggplant	String beans
Broccoli	Green pepper	Summer squash
Brussels sprouts	Kale	Tomatoes
Cabbage	Lettuce	Turnips
Carrots	Mushrooms	Zucchini
Cauliflower	Mustard greens	
Celery	Okra	

FRUITS

One serving equals 40 calories of fresh, frozen, or canned fruit without sugar. If it is packed in concentrated fruit juice, omit the juice. Frozen juices usually do not contain sugar, but read the label to check.

1 small apple
⅓ cup apple juice
½ cup applesauce (unsweetened)
2 medium fresh apricots
4 dried apricots
½ small banana
berries
    ½ cup blackberries, blueberries, or raspberries, or
    ¾ cup strawberries
10 large cherries
⅓ cup cider
cranberries (no limit if no sugar added)
2 dates
1 fresh fig

1 dried fig
½ grapefruit
½ cup grapefruit juice
¼ cup grape juice
12 grapes
½ small mango
melons
    ¼ small cantaloupe
    ⅛ medium honeydew
    1 cup watermelon
1 small nectarine
1 small orange
½ cup orange juice
¾ cup papaya
1 medium peach
1 small pear
1 medium persimmon
½ cup pineapple
⅓ cup pineapple juice
2 medium plums
2 medium prunes
¼ cup prune juice
2 tablespoons raisins
1 medium tangerine

WHOLE GRAINS

Whole-grain breads and cereals
Pita bread
Pastas (avoid those made from white flour; try whole-wheat or
    spinach noodles)
Brown rice
Barley
Bulgur
Legumes (lentils, beans, peas)
Millet
Oats
Wheat germ

To help you choose among the complex carbohydrates for your daily dietary limits, we've provided the following calorie-per-portion breakdown: 1 serving equals 70 calories, 15 grams of carbohydrate, and 2 grams of protein.

The following equal 1 serving:

    1 slice white, rye, raisin, or wheat bread
    1 small roll (16 rolls to the pound)
    1 ounce (saucer size) pita or Syrian bread

These rolls weigh about 2 ounces and are equal to 2 servings of starch (140 calories):

    Hamburger roll
    Frankfurter roll
    Bagel
    English muffin

These breads weigh ½ ounce a slice. Two slices are equal to 1 serving:

    Hollywood
    Weight Watchers
    Melba Thin (Arnold or Pepperidge Farm)

The following equal 1 serving of starch:

    1 tortilla
    1 matzoh (6-inch round)
    5 Melba toast rectangles
    8 Melba toast rounds (half-dollar size)
    25 unsalted pretzel sticks
    4 Uneeda Biscuits
    3 zwieback toast
    2 bread sticks (unsalted, 8 inches long)
    3 cups unsalted popcorn (no added fat)
    6 salt-free Venus Wafers
    4 arrowroot cookies
    3 ginger snaps
    5 vanilla wafers
    3 Lorna Doone shortbread cookies
    1½-inch square of angel food or sponge cake
    2 graham crackers
    ½ cup Jell-O (with sugar)
    2 tablespoons cornstarch
    2 tablespoons flour
    3 tablespoons cornflake crumbs
    1½ tablespoons uncooked barley
    ¼ cup graham cracker crumbs

¾ cup unfrosted cereal
¼ cup wheat germ
½ cup cooked cereal (unsalted)
½ cup dried beans or dried peas (cooked and unsalted)
⅓ cup whole-kernel frozen corn (unsalted or canned without salt or sugar)
1 (6-inch) ear of corn, no salt in the water
½ cup frozen lima beans (unsalted)
⅔ cup fresh parsnips (unsalted)
½ cup frozen peas (unsalted, frozen or canned without salt or sugar)
1 small unsalted potato (about size of tennis ball)
½ cup mashed potato (not instant, unsalted)
¾ cup fresh pumpkin (unsalted)
½ cup fresh or frozen winter squash (unsalted)
½ cup pasta (noodles, spaghetti, macaroni; unsalted)
½ cup cooked rice (unsalted)

The following foods contain more fat than other starches and more calories (about 115 calories per serving). They equal 1 starch and 1 fatty food per serving.

1 waffle or pancake (about size of saucer)
8 unsalted French-fried potatoes
1 small muffin (without salt or sugar)
1 small biscuit (without salt or sugar)

GOOD SNACK FOODS

Angel food cake, without icing
Arrowroot cookies
Fruit juice: grapefruit, apple, or orange
Fruits, especially bananas, which are high in potassium
Ginger snaps
Graham crackers
Lorna Doones
Matzoh
Melba toast
Popcorn, unsalted, unbuttered
Pretzels, unsalted only
Vanilla wafers
Whole-wheat crackers, unsalted
Zwieback toast

HIGH-SODIUM FOODS TO AVOID

Anchovies
Artichokes
Bacon
Barbecue sauces
Beets
Bouillon cubes
Brains
Canned fish, except that packed in water and low in salt
Catsup
Caviar
Celery salt and flakes
Chard
Cold cuts
Corn, taco, and tortilla chips
Corned beef
Duck sauce
Frankfurters
Frozen lima beans
Frozen peas
Garlic salt
Ham
Herring
Horseradish
Instant cocoa
Kale
Kidneys
Lox, or smoked salmon
Mayonnaise
Meat tenderizers
Molasses
Mustard
Olives
Onion salt
Pastrami
Pâté
Pickles
Potato chips
Preserved or pickled fish
Pretzels
Processed and fast foods
Relish

Sardines
Sauerkraut
Sausage
Soy sauce
Sturgeon
Sweet-and-sour sauces
Sweetbreads
Tomato juice
V-8 juice
White turnips
Worcestershire sauce

RECOMMENDED SUBSTITUTIONS

As our recipe section demonstrates, we recommend that women sharply restrict the amount of butter, cream, and salt in cooking, and substitute low-fat yogurt or tofu as the bases for mayonnaise and cream dressings and sauces.

Two

A Nutrient Inventory

With our increasingly busy and demanding lives, women can ill afford imbalanced diets or vitamin deficiencies. Becoming aware of the critical role played by the major vitamins, minerals, and other elements in building and maintaining our bodies is the first step toward good nutrition. Despite the increased emphasis on good health, nutritional eating, and exercise, millions of women continue to succumb to fad diets or fast foods, or suffer from eating disorders such as anorexia, bulimia, or binge eating. Others simply don't know how to put together healthy, balanced meals.

In this chapter we'll discuss the vitamins and minerals essential to good health—as well as some elements to avoid—explaining their role in the body's functions, identifying natural sources of these nutrients, and giving their recommended dietary allowances (RDA) suggested by the National Academy of Sciences. When it isn't possible to obtain the daily RDA of the essential nutrients from food alone, vitamin and mineral supplements can be used to make up the difference.

VITAMIN A

This vitamin, also called retinol, plays an important role in fighting off infections and helps prevent skin problems, abnormally heavy menstrual bleeding, and cancer. It also protects the layers of tissues that cover an organ, including skin and mucous membranes; aids the growth and maintenance of bones and teeth; and assures the correct function of the adrenal glands, which control responses to stress. Vitamin A also helps determine how fast your eyes adjust to darkness. Night blindness, in fact, is usually the first recognizable symptom that your vitamin A supply is not adequate. But long before a person would develop night blindness, anemia might occur, as the body's ability to deliver oxygen from the blood to the cells declines.

Many women need supplements of vitamin A when they suffer from menorrhagia, or heavy menstrual bleeding. While many of the women who suffer from this condition used to be encouraged to have hysterectomies, today physicians know that vitamin A can eliminate the problem. In one study, when 52 menorrhagic women were given 30,000 international units (IU) of vitamin A twice a day for thirty-five days, 23 reported the problem eliminated, 14 were improved, and 12 did not return for follow-up examination, usually an indication that the medication helped.

As we are becoming increasingly aware, vitamin A is also linked to fighting cancer, especially of the stomach, nasopharynx, and respiratory tract. The vitamin apparently battles cancer the same way it fends off infections—by heightening the functions of the immune defense system.

A vitamin A deficiency during pregnancy can have severe effects on a developing fetus, including cleft palate and kidney defects. Pregnant women should be careful to get adequate amounts of vitamin A for their baby's protection.

The recommended daily dietary allowance of vitamin A is 5,000 international units for men, 4,000 for women, 5,000 for pregnant women, 6,000 for lactating women, 1,400 for infants, and 2,000 to 3,300 for children. (The international unit is the standard form of measurement for some nutrients.)

Good sources of the vitamin are yellow and dark-green leafy vegetables, including carrots, spinach, kale, and broccoli, as well as tomatoes and egg yolk.

THE B COMPLEX

To be most effective and to prevent aggravating forms of anemia, the essential B vitamins must be taken together.

The B-complex vitamins—B_1, B_2, B_3, B_6, and B_{12}—are in the front line of the body's essential nutrients. Together, they play an important role in the production of energy, in central nervous system function, in the metabolism of carbohydrates and proteins, and in stimulation of the immune response. B_{12}, which contains cobalt, is essential to the formation of the nucleic acids RNA and DNA in the rapid regeneration of bone marrow and the production of red blood cells.

Foods containing the B vitamins include:

B_1 (thiamine) and B_2 (riboflavin)—liver and organ meats, pork, brewer's yeast, lean meats, eggs, green leafy vegetables, whole-grain breads and cereals, nuts and legumes

B_3 (niacin)—liver and organ meats, fish, tuna, dried peas and beans, whole grains, nuts, eggs

B_{12}—organ and muscle meats, milk, eggs, brewer's yeast, seafood (especially clams, oysters, and shrimp)

VITAMIN B_6

Pyridoxine, or vitamin B_6, eases the symptoms of many women's complaints of menstrual irregularities, premenstrual syndrome (PMS), depression, complications of pregnancy, and menstrual-phase acne, to name a few. It also plays a role in preventing heart disease, birth defects, and some childhood disorders. B_6 takes the edge off irritability and reduces fatigue and tension, and may reduce or eliminate breast swelling and headaches. It's not clear how or why B_6 has these effects. It acts on the central nervous system, which might affect the neurotransmitters dopamine and serotonin in the chain of actions that regulate the production of progesterone and other hormones. It may also aid in the liver's metabolism of estrogen.

B_6 might be viewed as the most valuable player of the B complex, a critical component in growth, repair of cells, and production of energy. It aids in the breakdown of the body's building blocks— amino acids—from ingested proteins, their synthesis from compounds within the body, their subsequent absorption into the cells, and their eventual formation into proteins. It also acts as a coenzyme in the formation of hemoglobin, the protein that carries oxygen from the lungs to each of the cells. (Hemoglobin circulates in the bloodstream.) Pyridoxine also is active in the metabolism of fats and carbohydrates. Without B_6 the body's cells could not produce energy.

A deficiency of B_6 first affects the nervous system, especially in children; in adults, especially women, it may result in depression. This is because the brain needs proteins to function, and with a B_6 deficiency the protein supply to the brain is greatly reduced. Since B_6 is involved in the metabolism of amino acids, as well as in the formation of the substance that holds them together—collagen—a deficiency not only interferes with repairs and growth but can result in serious structural damage to the gums, teeth, bones, and liver, and in a lowered immune response.

B_6 deficiency is not common, in part because the vitamin is stable to heat and acid; it's more resistant to food processing and storage than other vitamins and minerals. Adequate amounts of B_6 are usually obtained in a normal diet. Women taking oral contraceptives, however, commonly have B_6 deficiencies, marked by depression. Not all women become depressed when using oral contraceptives. And of those who do, the resulting depression is not necessarily due to pyridoxine deficiency. But among women on the pill who also have a B_6 deficiency, B_6 supplements can usually eliminate the depression. Some researchers have concluded that women with a history of depression, premenstrual depression, or depression during pregnancy—and who become worse after starting the pill—are most likely to respond to pyridoxine supplements. In one study, 220 out of 250 women responded to pyridoxine therapy for their depression. Oral contraceptives also interfere with the body's ability to metabolize carbohydrates and remove them from the bloodstream for storage in the liver. In some women, this side effect can create a state similar to diabetes. Supplements of B_6 help restore the glucose metabolism to a more normal range.

Nutritional sources of pyridoxine are liver and organ meats, whole-grain cereals and bread, wheat germ, soybeans, brewer's yeast, nuts, red meat, fish, spinach, avocados, bananas, green beens, green leafy vegetables, potatoes, molasses, cabbage, and green peppers. Vegetables should be eaten raw because cooking destroys the vitamin.

Some women with severe premenstrual symptoms and other problems—including depression—may need to supplement their diets to obtain adequate pyridoxine. It is available in supplements ranging from 5 to 500 milligrams; most over-the-counter vitamin supplements include 2 milligrams of B$_6$, the recommended daily allowance. There is no known toxicity of large doses of B$_6$, although it has been suggested by researchers that doses exceeding 2 grams per day may cause peripheral nerve damage. Overdoses from the normal diet are all but impossible. B$_6$ and the B-complex supplement should be taken with a meal to increase their absorption. Some women seem unable to tolerate B$_6$; they may become nauseated or dizzy with vitamin supplements. Researchers say this is usually because they've been given too high a dosage. Decreasing the dosage may resolve the problem.

B VITAMINS AND PMS

The involvement of B-complex vitamins in PMS was identified more than forty years ago, when some symptoms—nervous tension, anxiety, irritability, and mood swings—were observed in women with B-vitamin deficiencies. But the physician who reported this link noticed marked improvement in his patients after treatment with rice-bran extracts and brewer's yeast. Further research revealed that the liver could not deactivate estrogens when a B-vitamin deficiency existed. One theory suggests that an excess of estrogens in some women with PMS is caused by the inability of the liver to deactivate them due to B-vitamin deficiency. This theory meshes with recent findings that elevated blood estrogens in some PMS patients are active estrogens. The liver normally inactivates estrogens and the inactivated estrogens are cleared by the kidney in the urine.

The B-complex vitamins, especially B$_6$, relieve many of the symptoms associated with PMS in most women. Some women find that by carefully controlling their diet, emphasizing the foods that are good sources of B vitamins, their PMS symptoms are alleviated without vitamin supplements.

VITAMIN C

This is perhaps the most controversial of the vitamins, touted by some as the solution to a spectrum of maladies from the common cold, flu, infections, backaches, heart disease, mental illness, arthritis, infertility, fatigue, stress, diabetes, bone disease, cancer, to the toxic effects of pollutants. A heavy weight of medical research does support many of the contentions that vitamin C can ease or eliminate some of these conditions, especially heart disease, cancer, and diabetes. The debate over vitamin C and the common cold and other viral infections isn't likely to be settled in the near future.

What does this element actually do? Vitamin C, or ascorbic acid, has many vital functions in the body: helping metabolize amino acids; converting folic acid to its active form; forming collagen and other fibrous tissues that support the skin, tendons, bones, teeth, cartilage, and connective tissue. Virtually all the tissues in the body depend on vitamin C for proper growth, development, and maintenance. It is absorbed from the small intestine, circulated in the blood, and stored in the tissues. The glands—adrenals, thymus, pituitary, and corpus luteum—contain higher amounts than any other tissues. Its role in supporting the body's ability to withstand stress is evident from the fact that more vitamin C is concentrated in the adrenal glands than in any other organ, and that when the body is stressed in any way, high amounts of vitamin C are excreted in the urine. Interestingly, many of the symptoms of vitamin C deficiency, or scurvy, are identical to those of adrenal insufficiency: fatigue, muscle weakness, digestive disorders, and reduced ability to tolerate stress.

The absorption rate of vitamin C taken with iron is increased by as much as 1,000 percent. Vitamin C itself enhances the absorption of calcium and some essential amino acids, and inhibits the destruction of thiamine by tannin, which is found in tea.

The RDA for vitamin C ranges from 35 milligrams for infants to 60 milligrams for adults, 80 milligrams for pregnant women, and 100 milligrams for nursing mothers. Many of the research studies on vitamin C have used enormous dosages far in excess of the RDA. While there has been speculation about whether or not these large dosages are dangerous, researchers report that vitamin C is not toxic.

Good sources of ascorbic acid are citrus fruits and their juices, strawberries, cantaloupe, raw vegetables and fruits—including broccoli, cauliflower, kale, Brussels sprouts, peppers, parsley, turnip greens, cabbage, tomatoes, potatoes, and bean sprouts. The amount of sunlight absorbed by these foods as they grow determines their vitamin C content; more sunlight exposure produces more vitamin C.

CALCIUM

Calcium is the main structural mineral in the body, the building blocks of the skeleton, teeth, and soft tissues. Our need for calcium is constant because the skeleton is completely renewed every five years; if there isn't enough calcium available in the system when this rebuilding takes place, the bones will gradually thin out, become porous, and break easily. For women, the need for calcium is particularly great because of the changes our bodies undergo during pregnancy, nursing, menopause, and postmenopause.

About 99 percent of the body's 3 pounds of calcium is in the skeleton and teeth and is responsible for their hardness and strength. Calcium in the bones and teeth is not permanently stationed there, because the bones and teeth also serve as a reservoir for calcium. There is an almost constant exchange of calcium between the bones and the body fluids and soft tissues, where the rest of the calcium is located.

That 1 percent of the body's calcium outside the skeleton is also very important. It is essential for the strength of the intracellular membranes and for many important enzyme reactions involved in the clotting of blood and other processes; it regulates the excitability of peripheral nerves and muscles, so irritability is increased when calcium is low. Normal muscular contraction and relaxation, including the rhythm of the heart, depend on calcium.

Naturally, calcium is vitally important for growth and development. During the last trimester of pregnancy, between 200 and 300 milligrams of calcium is deposited every day in the skeleton of the fetus. Breast milk contains 250 to 500 milligrams of calcium each day. If a pregnant or lactating mother isn't supplying this calcium in her diet, most of it is going to come out of her bones, and the bone health of both mother and child will suffer.

Since the body maintains fairly constant blood levels of calcium, low levels occur only in very severe deficiencies. When a deficiency is bad, muscle spasms and convulsions usually occur. Insufficient dietary calcium can be a factor in rickets, osteomalacia, and osteoporosis. (See chapter 9.)

Besides its effects on bone mineralization and nerve and muscle irritability, calcium deficiency can also affect blood and tissue levels of two poisonous metals, lead and cadmium. When dietary calcium is low, the body retains more lead. This has been demonstrated in several experiments with both humans and animals.

The RDA for calcium ranges from a low of 360 milligrams (14 ounces of whole milk) for infants to a high of 1,200 milligrams (40 ounces of whole milk) for pregnant and lactating women. The RDA for adults, both men and women, is 800 milligrams but is expected to be increased to 1,000 milligrams soon in response to research studies. Researchers have found that the RDA of 800 milligrams is not enough to maintain positive calcium balance, and that most women do not ingest even the RDA. In addition, the average adult's loss of calcium through excretion totals 380 milligrams a day. (Calcium loss increases if excess quantities of protein or salt are ingested, or if caffeine, cigarettes, or alcohol are consumed in large quantities.) To maintain a positive calcium balance, at least 380 milligrams must be resupplied through the diet. However, all the calcium that is eaten is not absorbed. The average amount, researchers say, is 35 percent. So, in order to replace the average daily losses, almost 1,100 milligrams of calcium would have to be supplied every day. Of course the amount of calcium absorbed is not always 35 percent; it can range from 2 percent to 40 pecent. So even 1,100 milligrams might not be enough for many people; research indicates that even the current RDA is not adequate for much of the population.

One orthopedic researcher has reported that calcium absorption begins to diminish at age twenty; bone loss begins at age twenty-five, and supplementation should probably begin at that age to avoid osteoporosis.

The USDA found that consumption of calcium is generally 30 percent below the RDA in women over thirty-five. In women over forty-five, the average amount consumed was only 450 milligrams— almost 50 percent less than the RDA. Some researchers have clearly established that this amount is not sufficient to prevent loss of bone density. Calcium absorption becomes less efficient the older we get; as a result, osteoporosis has been considered to be a normal part of advancing age. But it can be prevented by diet and exercise, curtailing consumption of protein, salt, caffeine, alcohol, and stopping smoking.

Many other factors can contribute to a calcium deficiency. A high-protein diet, for example, causes more calcium to be excreted, thus raising the amount needed to maintain a positive calcium balance. High-fiber foods have been found to reduce calcium absorption. A small amount of fat in the intestine seems to improve calcium absorption; however, an excess of fat may form insoluble calcium soaps and sharply reduce absorption. Recent studies have also shown that refined white sugar causes a sharp increase in calcium excretion.

Several common drugs and over-the-counter medications inhibit calcium absorption or utilization. These include many antacids, tetracycline antibiotics, laxatives, diuretics, heparin, and anticonvulsant drugs.

The best source of calcium, not surprisingly, is mother's milk. Cow's milk is a good source of calcium, but not the only natural one, for adults and growing children. Egg yolk; fish (eaten with its bones); soybeans; green leafy vegetables, such as turnip greens, mustard greens, broccoli, and kale; roots, tubers, and seeds; and stews and soups made with bones can provide considerable calcium.

Some foods contain a lot of calcium but may not be good sources to rely on for your RDA. Some dark-green leafy vegetables, for example, including spinach, sorrel, parsley, Swiss chard, and beet greens, contain generous amounts of calcium but are also packed with oxalic acid, which inhibits the absorption of their calcium.

Because it is so difficult for the average person to get enough calcium from food alone, it is one nutrient that people are encouraged to take in supplements. Calcium supplements are available in a wide range of dose levels, from less than 100 milligrams to several hundred milligrams. Physicians recommend that younger women use supplements to bring their total calcium ingestion to 1,000 milligrams a day, while postmenopausal women should bring the level up to 1,500 milligrams a day.

Supplements of calcium are available in many forms—calcium carbonate, calcium gluconate, calcium lactate, and others. There is no general agreement about which form is the best. Among the products available are calcium-magnesium-zinc tablets by Thompson, oyster-shell products produced by Gray and Your Life, Caltrate 600 by Lederle, calcium carbonate by Plus, generic brands of calcium carbonate, and Tums, the antacid.

Don't forget that vitamin D is also necessary for calcium absorption and utilization, or that calcium is absorbed more effectively from food than from supplements. The 1,000 milligrams of calcium that most women need daily to provide the RDA and make up for the daily loss of calcium through excretion can be found in five 8-

ounce glasses of milk. Unfortunately, not many of us can drink that much milk without increasing our caloric intakes to unacceptably high levels.

CALCIUM CONCENTRATIONS IN FOOD (in milligrams)

Skim milk	8 oz.	302
2% milk	8 oz.	297
Whole milk	8 oz.	219
Buttermilk	8 oz.	285
Lowfat yogurt	1 cup	415
Lowfat yogurt w/fruit	1 cup	314
Frozen yogurt	1 cup	200
Cottage cheese	½ cup	116
Swiss cheese	1 oz.	272
Parmesan (grated)	1 oz.	390
Cheddar	1 oz.	204
Mozzarella	1 oz.	183
American cheese	1 oz.	174
Sardines w/bones	3 oz.	372
Salmon w/bones	3 oz.	285
Oysters	1 cup	226
Shrimp	1 cup	147
Bean curd	4 oz.	154
Collards	1 cup	357
Turnip greens	1 cup	267
Kale	1 cup	206
Mustard greens	1 cup	193
Dandelion greens	1 cup	147
Broccoli	1 cup	136
Bok choy	1 cup	116

Source: U.S. Department of Agriculture

THE CALCIUM-MAGNESIUM BALANCE

Americans, especially women, may also have a deficiency of magnesium in their diet. Magnesium helps calcium absorption and deposition in the bones, where it belongs. But calcium interferes with magnesium absorption. Magnesium decreases the demand for calcium and calcium increases the demand for magnesium. While it is critical for women to increase the amount of calcium in their diet, it is also important to watch the calcium-magnesium balance. This isn't easy, of course. You should favor foods that have at least as much magnesium as calcium, with a daily allowance of 300 to 600 milligrams of magnesium. Dairy products, for example, have ten times more calcium than magnesium.

Many women crave chocolate, which may be a sign of magnesium deficiency. Chocolate is relatively rich in magnesium and in phenylethylamine, a substance produced by the brain that is a cousin of amphetamine. Phenylethylamine is thought to be the chemical released into the bloodstream when people become infatuated or fall in love; researchers say this is one reason why some people "crave" chocolate—to get that falling-in-love high. Chocolate is one substance that many people with allergies must avoid; it has also been implicated as a catalyst of migraine headaches, hives, and upset stomachs. It also contains caffeine, although in much lower amounts than coffee or tea. An ounce of bittersweet chocolate contains 5 to 10 milligrams of caffeine, compared with 100 to 150 milligrams of caffeine in a cup of brewed coffee.

While their effects may not be the same, there are far better sources of magnesium than chocolate: green leafy vegetables, legumes, nuts, seeds, shellfish, cereals, and whole grains.

The following chart can help you identify whole grains and vegetables with higher calcium-magnesium ratios. Foods with relatively low calcium-magnesium ratios aren't necessarily bad, of course. Lettuce, for example, has a ratio of just 0.26 yet it's a vitamin-rich, low-calorie, healthful food that is good to include in your daily menus.

CONCENTRATIONS OF CALCIUM AND MAGNESIUM IN FOOD

	Magnesium (mg./100 cal.)	Calcium (mg./100 cal.)	Calcium/ Magnesium Ratio
Spinach	315	365.0	0.86
Cabbage	76	200.0	0.38
Carrots	55	82.0	0.67
Tomato	64	61.0	1.00
Lettuce	63	238.0	0.26
Potato	45	9.0	5.00
Lentils	24	24.0	1.00

	Magnesium (mg./100 cal.)	Calcium (mg./100 cal.)	Calcium/ Magnesium Ratio
Cashews	48	7.0	7.00
Almonds	45	39.0	1.20
Brazil nuts	38	28.0	1.40
Hazel nuts	36	33.0	1.10
Peanuts	30	12.0	2.40
Chestnuts	21	14.0	1.50
Walnuts	20	15.0	1.34
Pecans	19	11.0	1.80
Sunflower seeds	7	21.0	0.30
Rye	34	11.5	3.00
Wheat	34	11.0	3.10
Oat	38	18.0	2.10
Corn	42	6.0	7.00
Brown rice	25	9.0	2.80
Barley	11	4.6	2.30
Millet	50	6.2	8.20
Buckwheat	69	34.0	2.00

Source: U.S. Department of Agriculture

VITAMIN D

Vitamin D is required for calcium to be absorbed from the intestines. Vitamin D consumed in foods such as fortified milk, liver, tuna, and salmon and produced in the skin after exposure to the sun is an inactive form. To affect calcium absorption, it must first be changed into the active vitamin D hormone by the liver and kidneys. As people age, their ability to activate vitamin D lessens. Additionally, older people are deficient in vitamin D because they usually consume few foods that contain it and are rarely out in the sun. Without enough of the vitamin D hormone, calcium in the diet is of limited value because it is not absorbed by the body.

POTASSIUM

Potassium, one of the most abundant minerals in the body, is critical to muscular contraction and nerve stimulation; it also regulates the body's water balance. Athletes, in particular, must be careful to maintain adequate potassium levels; sweating during workouts can cause the salt and potassium levels in the body to drop. Inadequate potassium may lead to muscle cramping; if levels fall dramatically low, ventricular fibrillation, in which the heart vibrates rather than pumps, can occur and cause sudden death. Muscle weakness, deterioration, and periodic paralysis from potassium deficiency are quite common. The body's concentration of potassium is regulated by the kidneys and requires a proper balance with sodium (salt). Muscle and nerve functioning suffer when there is an imbalance between sodium and potassium. An excess of one will cause the loss of the other in the urine. Many coaches urge their athletes to drink Gatorade, a tart beverage with a balanced potassium-salt formula, to prevent cramping. Diets high in salt lead to potassium deficiency. Women who take diuretics to prevent fluid retention, bloating, and weight gain before their periods may well be depleting their potassium reserves. Individuals with high blood pressure, diabetes, or liver disease also are high risks for potassium deficiency.

Bananas, oranges, orange juice, broccoli, lettuce, melons, wheat germ, unsalted peanuts, lentils, dates, potatoes, and squash are good sources of potassium. Hypoglycemia may result in a loss of potassium. Potassium requirements can be increased by many other factors, including alcoholism, renal disease, anorexia, vomiting, and gastric problems. Drugs that can cause potassium deficiency include diuretics, penicillin, insulin, silver nitrate, corticosteroids, purgatives, laxatives, ammonium chloride, amphoterin, glucagon, aminosalicylic acid, carbenoxolone, and carbenicillin. Acute stress, trauma, or surgery can also cause a sudden deficit in potassium, as does exercise or work that causes the body to sweat.

There is no official recommended daily allowance for potassium, but experts say potassium intake should equal salt intake, or 2.6 grams a day. Potassium lost through sweat will not be made up for by this 2.6 grams, however. Athletes and those who work up a sweat might need 3 to 6 grams a day. Be aware, however, that too much potassium can be toxic. Acute toxicity occurs with daily doses of 25 grams a day, which can cause cardiac arrhythmia, weakness, anxiety, low blood pressure, confusion, and loss of sensation in the extremities.

ZINC

Of all the minerals in the body, zinc is one of the most important and most neglected. It plays a major role in the synthesis of proteins and DNA and RNA; it is required for cell growth and the formation of connective tissues; it is a factor in forty or more enzyme reactions. Without zinc, for example, the carbon dioxide exchange in the cells could not be accomplished fast enough to keep a human alive. Zinc acts as the traffic cop of the cells and surrounding membranes, policing the metabolism of other minerals, including copper, magnesium, manganese, and selenium. Since zinc is necessary for cell growth, any tissue that depends on rapid cell proliferation will suffer the effects of a deficiency first and most severely. A zinc deficiency can cause delayed healing of injuries; deformities of offspring; impaired development of bones, muscles, and the nervous system; delayed sexual maturity; and other problems.

An excess of copper in the system can lead to zinc deficiency. In the United States, most drinking water passes through copper plumbing pipes, most over-the-counter vitamin supplements contain copper but not zinc, and freshly grown fruits and vegetables are harvested from soil severely deficient in zinc. Zinc deficiency is a common condition in women, especially those with copper IUDs. Some researchers report that the level of copper is high and that of zinc is low one week before the menstrual period, when women are more liable to depressive disorders. Zinc levels can also be disturbed by estrogen, which is why women taking oral contraceptives may have zinc-related problems. Also, diuretics deplete zinc levels. If you take water pills for salt retention, you may require zinc supplements.

Zinc is also involved in the body's response to stress. In animal experiments, zinc supplements have greatly reduced the number of stress ulcers produced. In human studies, blood levels of zinc have been found to rise considerably in anticipation of stress and during the stress itself (such as surgery). Excretion of zinc increases by a factor of 3 to 5 during stress, another indication that the body prepares to deal with stress by increasing the amount of zinc that is available to tissues for healing or other purposes.

The best sources of zinc are liver, mushrooms, milk, eggs, red meat, brewer's yeast, nuts, legumes, and seafood, especially oysters and herring. The recommended daily requirement is 15 milligrams for adults, 20 milligrams for pregnant women, and 25 milligrams for lactating women.

CAFFEINE

Caffeine is found in coffee, tea, most colas and soda drinks, and chocolate. Women in particular should reduce the amount of caffeine in their diet because it may increase the body's need for B vitamins; it makes breast symptoms—breast swelling, engorgement, and tenderness—worse; it blocks absorption of calcium by the body; and it has been identified as a risk factor in heart disease and cancer. It may increase irritability, hyperactivity, and headaches. Many women find that if they reduce or eliminate caffeine, one or more of their symptoms will improve, some to a very significant degree. Even those whose symptoms do not go away find some improvement.

SALT

Salt is one of the earliest chemicals, used by humans since prehistoric times. In more recent times, salt has come to be portrayed as a villain in our foods, the exacerbator of hypertension, heart and kidney disease, stroke, and other conditions. More than 60 million Americans suffer from high blood pressure, or hypertension. This condition usually produces no symptoms until sudden signs of permanent organ damage appear and chronic illness develops or the person suffers a heart attack or stroke and dies. Between 15 and 20 percent of the population carry the genetic predisposition to hypertension and should try to eliminate salt from their diet or restrict it to 5 grams a day or less. You can give up salt without giving up flavor; as you will see, condiments, herbs, and spices such as onions, garlic, pepper, mustard, and lemon juice can make you wholly forget salt.

It is particularly important for women to avoid salt because it causes fluid retention, one of the most frequent complaints of women before and during menstruation. Women who experience swelling of the face, hands, feet, or breasts, or weight gain in the days preceding their periods should try to eliminate salt from their diet, especially prior to menstruation.

Studies of women suffering from fluid retention have shown that they have elevated levels of hormones of the adrenal glands, which control water and salt retention by the kidney. These salt-retaining hormones are stimulated when stress and high brain serotonin trigger the release of a brain hormone called ACTH. Excess refined carbohydrates increase brain serotonin. And insulin also plays a role. Excess refined carbohydrates trigger insulin release in excess. Insulin is known to prevent the kidneys from excreting salt. Salt and water retention is in part an insulin effect. For many women, a monthly craving for sweets and subsequent ingestion of large amounts of refined carbohydrates or sugar precede the swelling in their premenstrual phases; subsequent weight gain seems to confirm the roles of refined sugar–triggered insulin release. Poor nutrition decreases resistance to stress. By itself, stress causes the adrenal glands to release in the blood increased amounts of salt-retaining hormones, which only worsen the salt-retaining effect of insulin.

About two-thirds of the salt ingested by Americans comes from processed foods; the rest is naturally present in natural foods and water. A *Consumer Reports* study showed that there are surprising hidden sources of salt: ½ cup of prepared Jell-O Instant Pudding has 404 milligrams of sodium, more sodium than 3 slices of Oscar Mayer sugar-cured bacon at 302 milligrams; 2 slices of Pepperidge Farm white bread contain more sodium than one ounce of Lay's Potato Chips; 1 ounce of Kellogg's Corn Flakes has almost twice the amount of salt as an ounce of Planters cocktail peanuts. Over-the-counter medications too are offenders. A single dose of Alka-Seltzer carries 521 milligrams of salt, a dose of Bromo Seltzer has 717 milligrams, and Sal-Hepatica contains 1,000 milligrams.

Among fast-food restaurant offerings, the sodium content is extremely high:

Food	Amount	Sodium (in milligrams)
McDonald's Big Mac	1	1,510
Burger King Whopper	1	909
Burger Chef hamburger	1	393
Kentucky Fried Chicken (original recipe)	3 pieces	2,285
McDonald's Egg McMuffin	1	914
Dairy Queen Brazier Dog	1	868
McDonald's apple pie	1	414
Burger King vanilla shake	1	159
McDonald's chocolate shake	1	329

The American Heart Association, in its booklet *Cooking Without Your Salt Shaker* (available from its local chapters), suggests the following seasonings for foods instead of salt:

MEATS

Beef	Bay leaf, dry mustard powder, green pepper, marjoram, fresh mushrooms, nutmeg, onion, pepper, sage, thyme
Chicken	Lemon juice, green pepper, sage, thyme, paprika, parsley, fresh mushrooms, marjoram, poultry seasoning
Fish	Lemon juice, paprika, bay leaf, curry powder, dry mustard powder, green pepper, marjoram, fresh mushrooms
Lamb	Curry powder, garlic, mint, mint jelly, pineapple, rosemary
Pork	Apple, applesauce, garlic, onion, sage
Veal	Apricot, bay leaf, curry powder, ginger, marjoram, oregano

VEGETABLES

Asparagus	Garlic, lemon juice, onion, vinegar
Corn	Green pepper, pimiento, fresh tomato
Cucumbers	Chives, dill, garlic, vinegar
Green beans	Dill, lemon juice, marjoram, nutmeg, pimiento
Greens	Onion, pepper, vinegar
Peas	Green pepper, mint, fresh mushrooms, onion, parsley
Potatoes	Green pepper, mace, onion, paprika, parsley
Rice	Chives, green pepper, onion, pimiento, saffron
Squash	Brown sugar, cinnamon, ginger, mace, nutmeg, onion
Tomatoes	Basil, marjoram, onion, oregano

Three

The Focus
on Fiber

*G*randparents—and even parents—used to say that "roughage" was good for us. Roughage seems to have disappeared from the American vocabulary, but a distinct hue and cry has been heard in the land about something called fiber. Fiber is good for you. What a coincidence. That's just what our grandparents and parents used to say before the word *fiber* was in vogue.

Natural carbohydrates—starches are complex carbohydrates, sugars are simple carbohydrates—are the only source of a non-nutrient called dietary fiber. Fiber is a carbohydrate found in plants that cannot be digested by human beings. It provides bulk to the diet, which eases the digestive and waste-removal process. After it's ingested, fiber passes through the human digestive tract relatively intact. Along the way, it absorbs a lot of other substances, binds to some toxic and potentially carcinogenic elements resting in the intestinal system, and removes them as waste from the body. Acting something like a chimney sweep inside a brick fireplace, fiber cleans the body out. In doing so, it prevents many stomach and intestinal disorders, and is thought to help prevent colon and rectal cancer, hemorrhoids, intestinal diseases, and other conditions. As our forebears said, fiber is good for you.

Some fiber substances are digested by bacteria in the gut and then absorbed by the body. But, all in all, dietary fiber provides few or relatively few calories. Excellent sources of fiber are whole grains, legumes, fruits, and vegetables.

Carbohydrates are broken down by the digestive system into simple sugars, one of which is glucose, the molecule of life. Low-carbohydrate diets are dangerous because glucose is the body's main energy source. It is the fuel that feeds the brain; it is the main fuel for muscles. Without carbohydrates, your body is forced to run on fats and protein, a potentially dangerous situation. Fats burn insufficiently in the absence of carbohydrates, with the result that the blood becomes polluted with the fat waste product called ketone bodies. These are toxic compounds that can damage the brain and cause nausea, fatigue, and apathy. When your body must rely on proteins for energy, this vital nutrient is then not available for building and replacing body tissues.

We need more carbohydrates. They can actually help you lose weight, for many reasons. There are more vitamins and minerals and trace nutrients in carbohydrates than in fats and proteins. Complex carbohydrates, that is, starches, fruits, and vegetables, fulfill the physical as well as psychological need for food. They make you feel as though you've eaten something, they fill your stomach, and in the case of fruits, they satisfy your craving for sweets.

Fiber is a special kind of carbohydrate. It is not considered an essential nutrient. Human beings can survive without any fiber in their diets, and insufficient fiber does not produce a classic deficiency disease. But it is possible that many ailments that afflict humans in developed nations are signs of a dietary shortage of fiber.

The current rage for fiber started in 1970 with the publication of a medical study by a renowned British physician, Dr. Denis Burkitt. He reported that in nations where the average diet includes large amounts of fiber (such as Japan), the incidence of various diseases is remarkably low: cancer of the colon and rectum, diverticulosis and other intestinal disorders, heart disease, hemorrhoids, hiatus hernia, appendicitis, gallstones, and varicose veins. All these conditions are common in Western countries, where the diet is typically low in fiber.

One of fiber's primary roles is to act as an expediter of waste removal from the body. It absorbs many times its weight in water, acting like a sponge in the large intestine to make stools easier to pass. Thus it works to prevent constipation. It also binds to substances in the intestinal tract and removes them from the body quickly; in particular it binds to carcinogenic and toxic substances.

In so doing, fiber helps prevent various types of cancer and intestinal disorders that are caused by bacteria feeding upon food sitting in the intestinal tract.

Fiber is also a diet aid. Obesity is rare in populations where a lot of starchy carbohydrates, complete with their natural fiber, are consumed. But excess weight is a common problem in this country and the Western world, where people consume low-fiber diets. The more fiber your diet contains, the fewer calories you're likely to consume. Fiber itself yields few, if any, calories, and many fibrous foods, especially fruits and vegetables, are themselves low in calories. Since fiber absorbs water as it passes through the digestive tract, fiber is filling. You're more likely to feel satisfied by a high-fiber meal before you have a chance to overeat. It also takes a long time to chew most fibrous foods. This slows down the process of eating, allowing time for the signs of satiety to reach your brain before you've overeaten. The process of chewing makes you feel like you've eaten something substantial. And although fiber does contribute some calories (through the fatty acids produced by gut bacteria), it also may reduce the number of calories your body absorbs from the other foods you eat. Possibly because of the decrease in "gut transit time" (the time it takes for food to be digested and excreted) caused by fiber, small amounts of the fat and protein you eat are excreted as waste instead of being absorbed through the small intestine. Therefore, a few of the calories you eat really "don't count."

There are many kinds of fiber. The most common types of fiber in our diet are cellulose, hemicellulose, bran, pectins, gums, mucilages, and lignins; the most common sources of these fibers are whole grains, fruits, and vegetables.

You shouldn't rely on only one source of fiber in your diet; the health value of different fibers varies. Bran is not the total answer. (Bran interferes with the absorption of some minerals by the body, and the amount you ingest should be limited.) In fact, overconsumption of one type of fiber can be harmful.

FIBER IN FOOD

Food	Serving	Fiber (*in grams*)
Graham crackers	2	1.5
Rye bread	1 slice	2.0

Food	Serving	Fiber (in grams)
Whole-wheat bread	1 slice	2.4
All-Bran cereal	1 cup	23.0
Bran Buds	¾ cup	18.0
Grape-Nuts	⅓ cup	5.0
Rolled oats, dry	½ cup	4.5
Shredded wheat	2 biscuits	6.1
Apple	1 small	3.1
Applesauce	½ cup	1.7
Banana	1 medium	1.8
Cantaloupe	¾ cup	1.4
Cherries	10	0.8
Grapefruit	½	2.6
Grapes	16	0.4
Orange	1 small	1.8
Peach	1 medium	1.3
Pear	1 medium	2.8
Plum	2 small	1.6
Strawberries	½ cup	2.6
Tangerine	1 medium	2.1
Broccoli, cooked	¾ cup	1.6
Cabbage, cooked	¾ cup	2.2
Cabbage, raw	1 cup	2.1
Carrots, cooked	¾ cup	2.1
Carrots, raw	1 medium	3.7
Cauliflower, cooked	½ cup	1.2
Cauliflower, raw	1 cup	1.8
Celery	2½ stalks	3.0
Corn	⅔ cup	4.2
Green beans	½ cup	1.2
Kale, cooked	½ cup	2.0
Lentils, cooked	½ cup	4.0
Lettuce	1 cup	0.8
Peas, cooked	½ cup	3.8
Potatoes, cooked	⅔ cup	3.1
Brown rice, cooked	1 cup	1.1
White rice, cooked	1 cup	0.4
Spinach	2 large leaves	1.8

Source: High Carbohydrate and Fiber Research Foundation, Lexington, Kentucky

The leading sources of fiber in general are the following:

- Legumes, dried beans, and peas, including baked beans, kidney beans, split peas, dried limas, chick-peas (garbanzos), pinto beans, and black beans
- Bran cereals, including Bran Buds and All-Bran; also good are 100% Bran, Raisin Bran, Most, Cracklin' Oat Bran, and Fruitful Bran
- Fresh or frozen lima beans, baby limas and Fordhook limas
- Fresh or frozen green peas
- Dried fruit, with figs, apricots, and dates the best sources
- Raspberries, blackberries, and strawberries
- Sweet corn
- Whole-wheat and whole-grain cereals and products, including rye, oats, buckwheat, and stoneground cornmeal; rely on bread, muffins, pastas, pizzas, and pancakes made with these flours
- Broccoli
- Baked potatoes (with the skin); mashed and boiled potatoes are also good sources
- Green beans
- Plums, pears, and apples are high in pectin and have edible skins, which increase the fiber content
- Raisins and prunes
- Dark-green leafy vegetables, including spinach, beet greens, kale, chard, collard greens, and turnip greens
- Nuts, especially almonds, Brazil nuts, peanuts, and walnuts
- Cherries
- Bananas
- Carrots
- Coconut
- Brussels sprouts

Food should be your source of fiber; adults need about 40 grams a day of dietary fiber from all sources. The benefits of fiber can be obtained by improving your diet overall, not by relying on additives. Substituting high-fiber complex carbohydrates—whole grains, cereals, legumes, fruits, and vegetables—for fats and processed foods should accomplish this goal. Raw fruits and vegetables have more fiber than cooked or processed versions, and whole grains are preferable to finer versions. Drink lots of water to help your body utilize the fiber.

Four

Straight from the Heart

*H*eart disease, one of the leading killers of Americans, is called a men's disease by physicians. Men are four times more likely than women to have a fatal heart attack; for one-fourth of the victims, a fatal attack is the first clinical sign of the disease. Women, on the other hand, seem protected from coronary heart disease and related disorders by the hormone estrogen. Logically enough, the incidence of heart attacks increases in women after menopause, when estrogen is no longer secreted by the ovaries.

Estrogen apparently increases a protein in your bloodstream called HDL, for high-density lipoprotein. HDL is called a cholesterol scavenger because it removes cholesterol from the cells and takes it to the liver for excretion. Researchers associate high levels of HDL in the blood with a low risk of heart disease, and low levels with a high risk.

To understand HDL, you have to know something about cholesterol. Cholesterol is a form of fat found in the bloodstream. The cells need a certain amount of cholesterol. It forms part of their walls (membranes). The manufacture of sex hormones also requires cholesterol. But too much of it results in the formation of thick, fatty deposits on the walls of blood vessels that restrict blood flow and make the heart work harder. Cholesterol is unable to travel in the blood by itself. It requires a carrier. The kind of carrier that moves it determines whether cholesterol will be removed from cells and taken to the liver for excretion (as HDL does) or whether it will be taken to a cell and stored. LDL, or low-density lipoprotein, carries cholesterol to the cells and is therefore a risk factor for heart disease.

High levels of LDL and low levels of HDL mean that more cholesterol is being deposited in the cells than is being carried off. That permits fat to accumulate on the membranes. This greatly enhances a woman's chances of having a heart attack or any other atherosclerotic type of heart disease.

Women whose ovaries are still secreting estrogen are likely to have higher levels of HDL and lower risk of heart disease than women past menopause and men. Other factors that indicate a low risk of heart disease are good heredity, low body weight, and regular exercise. Strenuous exercise increases HDL cholesterol and may be part of the reason such exercise protects against heart disease.

Despite the fact that the body makes all the cholesterol we need—1,000 milligrams a day—the average American takes in 600 milligrams a day of cholesterol over and above that which the liver makes. Cholesterol is made from fat. More than the cholesterol you eat, the amount of cholesterol circulating in your blood is influenced by the amount and kinds of fats you consume. Specifically, diets rich in saturated fats tend to raise the level of LDL cholesterol, while polyunsaturated fats tend to lower it. All animal fats contain cholesterol; no cholesterol is present in any vegetable foods.

The vast majority of Americans have too much LDL cholesterol. The more cholesterol there is in our blood, the greater the likelihood that some will build up on the inner walls of our arteries as plaques of atherosclerosis. As the plaques get larger and larger, the opening through which the blood must flow gets narrower and narrower. Eventually a small clot could completely shut down circulation through an artery. If the artery happens to be one that nourishes the heart, this life-sustaining muscle is suddenly deprived of essential oxygen and cannot work; a heart attack is the result. Similar blockage in an artery feeding the brain can result in stroke.

The importance of diet in heart disease seems clear. In Mediterranean countries like Greece and Italy, where the population cooks generously with vegetable oil and uses heavy oil-based dressings and sauces, the incidence of coronary heart disease is far lower than in the United States. Researchers think that is because olive oil, which is polyunsaturated and lacks cholesterol, is used. In Japan, only 10 percent of the diet is fat; most of that is polyunsaturated fat from vegetable sources. The death rate from coronary artery disease is just 20 out of 10,000 in Japan, less than half the U.S. rate.

Reducing blood cholesterol levels through diet is important. It is smart to eat foods lower in fat and limit your cholesterol intake to 300 milligrams or less a day.

CHOLESTEROL IN FOOD

Food	Portion	Cholesterol (in milligrams)
Bacon	2 slices	15
Beef (lean)	3 oz.	77
Frankfurter	2	112
Ham, boiled	2 oz.	51
Kidney (beef)	3 oz.	315
Lamb (lean)	3 oz.	85
Liver (beef)	3 oz.	372
Pork (lean)	3 oz.	75
Veal (lean)	3 oz.	84
Chicken (dark meat, no skin)	3 oz.	77
Chicken (white meat, no skin)	3 oz.	65
Eggs (whole, or yolk only)	1 large	252
Turkey (dark, no skin)	3 oz.	86
Turkey (white, no skin)	3 oz.	65
Clams, raw	3 oz.	43
Crab, canned	3 oz.	85
Flounder	3 oz.	69
Haddock	3 oz.	42
Halibut	3 oz.	50
Lobster	3 oz.	71
Mackerel	3oz.	84
Oysters, raw	3 oz.	42
Salmon, canned	3 oz.	30
Sardines	3 oz.	119
Scallops	3 oz.	45
Shrimp, canned	3 oz.	128
Tuna, canned	3 oz.	55

Food	Portion	Cholesterol (in milligrams)
Butter	1 tbsp.	35
Buttermilk	1 cup	5
Cheese, cottage (4% fat)	½ cup	24
Cheese, cottage (1% fat)	½ cup	12
Cheese, cream	1 oz.	31
Cheese, hard	1 oz.	24–28
Cheese spread	1 oz.	18
Chocolate milk (low-fat)	1 cup	20
Cream, heavy	1 tbsp.	21
Ice cream	½ cup	27
Ice milk	½ cup	13
Milk, skim	1 cup	5
Milk, 1% fat	1 cup	14
Milk, 2% fat	1 cup	22
Milk, whole	1 cup	34
Yogurt (low-fat)	1 cup	17
Angel food cake	1 slice	0
Cornbread	1 ounce	58
Lemon meringue pie	⅛ of 9-in. pie	98
Muffin, plain	3-in. diameter	21
Egg noodles	1 cup	50
Pancakes	3 medium pancakes	54
Sponge cake	1/12 of 10-in. cake	162

In developing a low-fat, low-cholesterol diet, you should:

Limit high-cholesterol foods like eggs and organ meats.
Eat no more than three egg yolks a week, including those used in cooking.
Use only lean cuts of meat.
Eat skinless chicken and turkey and fish, which are lower in fat than other meats.
Use margarine instead of butter.
Drink skim or low-fat milk instead of whole milk.
Add dried beans, fruits with pectins (such as apples), and

whole grains to your diet. Some studies show that all these foods help lower blood cholesterol.

High-fiber diets may do an even more efficient job of lowering cholesterol levels than do low-fat diets, according to recent medical studies. Fiber is the undigested residue of fruits and vegetables that actually absorbs fat in the digestive tract, blocks the absorption of glucose, and speeds the removal of waste from the body. There are three types of fiber: vegetable, bran, and chemically purified. Bran, which is more than 90 percent cellulose, has no beneficial effect on cholesterol levels. But chemically purified fiber, including pectins (found in most fruits), guar gum (found in beans), and the fiber in rolled oats and carrots (cellulose) can bring about a significant lowering of cholesterol.

We should strive for meals that are low in fat, low in salt, and high in fiber. This provides the best dietary protection and is the basis of the American Heart Association's recommended eating plan.

CALCIUM AND HEART DISEASE

Calcium may also play a role in heart-disease prevention and treatment. In one study, where individuals were given calcium supplements of 750 milligrams a day, bone density was maintained or increased and blood levels of cholesterol were also reduced. Other studies of calcium supplements found lower blood concentrations of both cholesterol and triglycerides by as much as 25 percent. Another study found that calcium specifically lowered the LDL cholesterol.

OTHER RISK FACTORS

Diet is not the only risk factor involved in heart disease, of course. There are other issues that women should be concerned with in preventing heart disease.

Heredity. Genes play a critical role in determining whether or not you'll develop heart disease. While you can't do much about them, you should know that a family history of heart disease affects males more than females. But if you have any of the other risk factors *and* a family history of the condition, beware. You should be extremely careful about your diet and physical condition. Above all, don't smoke.

Smoking. Smoking damages the blood vessels, and fat accumulates on damaged vessels more easily. Smoking also increases carboxyhemoglobin (where carbon monoxide replaces oxygen) and encourages the release of catecholamines (which are natural body chemicals that make the heart beat faster), both of which put extra stress on the heart by depriving it of oxygen and increasing demands on outflow. Those women who smoke one pack of cigarettes a day have a three times greater risk of a heart attack than a nonsmoking woman. Those who smoke two packs a day have five times the risk.

Diabetes. If you developed diabetes as an adult and primarily because you are overweight to the point of obesity, or if a glucose-tolerance test indicates you are a potential diabetic, controlling the disease is critical. Your chances of having coronary heart disease are twenty times greater than your nondiabetic counterpart's, which makes diabetes a far greater risk factor in women than smoking. This type of diabetes is almost always associated with obesity, and weight loss can almost completely control the disease and improve your overall health.

Obesity. Obesity in itself is not a risk factor in heart disease, even though being very overweight strains the heart. A healthy heart, however, can compensate for significant amounts of excess weight only up to a certain age without apparent sign of breakdown. But obesity is a major risk factor for other diseases that are, in turn, risk factors for heart disease. Almost all adult female diabetics are obese, and many obese women have high triglyceride and cholesterol levels along with low HDL levels. Those who are overweight usually tend not to exercise much.

Hypertension. High blood pressure can exist alone or be accompanied by obesity. It is measured in pressure units. The top number means the amount of work the heart has to do to pump blood through the arteries. The bottom number denotes the backflow or elasticity of the arteries. The upper limits of normal for the systolic pressure (top number) for women over forty is considered 140 to 150. The top limit for normal diastolic pressure (bottom number) is 90 to 94; 80 is considered normal for many adults. Mild hypertension (a diastolic pressure of 90 to 95) is probably not an important risk factor in coronary heart disease and is usually reversible by consuming less salt or by losing weight if you are overweight.

Lack of exercise. People who exercise regularly usually have higher levels of HDL than their sedentary counterparts. Exercise is also a preventive of many ailments. Ideally, you should exercise at least twenty minutes three times a week. If you have never exercised before, and especially if you are over forty, start with brisk walking for at least an hour at a time. Before beginning any exercise program more strenuous than this, consult your physician.

Five

An Anti-Cancer Strategy

*C*ancer. It's a word that evokes fear and concern in almost everyone. Many elements in the air, in water, in household products—even in the workplace—are carcinogenic, and many people have a genetic predisposition to certain cancers because relatives have been afflicted with them. While the risk of cancer is impossible to eliminate entirely, researchers now know that there are many more ways to reduce the risk of the disease than simply to quit smoking.

As medical researchers around the world have uncovered links between diet and cancer, the Committee on Diet, Nutrition, and Cancer of the National Academy of Sciences has issued reports recommending that everyone increase the amount of fruits and vegetables they eat. In choosing fruits and vegetables, the committee strongly suggested that we increase our intake of those containing vitamin A—particularly a form of vitamin A known as beta-carotene—in order to gain protection against some forms of cancer.

There are three types of vitamin A:

- Carotene or beta-carotene, the primary kind of vitamin A found in fruits and vegetables
- Carotenoids, also found in fruits and vegetables, are a minor source of vitamin A
- Retinol, found in meats and their byproducts

Carotene or beta-carotene is the form of vitamin A that is believed to provide the best protection against cancer.

46

Nutrition and cancer experts working separately in this country and overseas in more than a dozen projects found that diets rich in carotene offered protection against some forms of cancer. The strongest evidence is of its preventive properties against cancer of the lung, stomach, and esophagus, but some studies also show that it provides some protection against cancer of the mouth, colon, rectum, prostate, and bladder. A Chicago study reported only 2 cases of lung cancer among 500 men, including some smokers, who ate many fruits and vegetables rich in vitamin A; that incidence contrasted to 14 lung cancer cases among 500 men who ate few of these foods. Norwegian researchers found that men who ate many vegetables rich in vitamin A experienced only one-third as much lung cancer as those eating little of these foods. In Japan, scientists reported 30 pecent fewer cases of lung cancer among people who ate vegetables rich in vitamin A every day; their study group also had lower rates of stomach cancer.

One simple way to spot high-carotene foods at the produce stand and supermarket is to look for deep-green and yellow vegetables and fruits. These are the ones with lots of vitamin A; the deep-green or yellow variety of a particular vegetable usually contains many times more vitamin A than the lighter color. Romaine lettuce contains four times as much vitamin A as iceberg lettuce; green asparagus provides ten times as much vitamin A as white asparagus; green beans have more vitamin A than wax beans.

The nutrition experts at the National Academy of Sciences have not specified how much vitamin A we should include in our diet in order to fight off cancer cells. But nutritionists generally say we should include 4 servings of fruits and vegetables a day, with 2 or 3 of them of foods rich in vitamin A. It's a commonsense approach that is wise to follow.

Simply substituting some foods for others may be one way to increase the amount of vitamin A in your diet. Try to eat a green salad based on romaine lettuce every day, or add tomatoes, green pepper, or carrots to the salad you already make, or to sauces and stews that you prepare. For snacks, keep carrot sticks, slices of green pepper, broccoli, or cauliflower handy as finger foods; these crudités are preferable substitutes for nuts, chips, or other hors d'oeuvres at parties. When you want something sweet, try making pies, breads, muffins, or cakes from pumpkin, zucchini, or sweet potatoes.

CAROTENE IN FOOD

Best Sources*	Moderate†	Low‡
Apricots	Brussels sprouts	Apple
Asparagus	Yellow corn	Banana
Broccoli	Green beans	Cabbage
Cantaloupe	Green pepper	Cauliflower
Carrots	Peas	Celery
Dark-green leafy vegetables	Summer squash	Cherries
Kale	Watermelon	Cucumber
Mango		Grapes
Peach		Grapefruit
Pumpkin		Iceberg lettuce
Romaine lettuce		Kohlrabi
Spinach		Lemon
Sweet potato		Lime
Tomato		Orange
Winter squash		Pear
		Pineapple
		Plum
		White potato
		Raspberries
		Strawberries
		Tangerines

Source: National Academy of Sciences Committee on Diet, Nutrition, and Cancer
* More than 1,000 IU of vitamin A per serving
† 500 to 1,000 IU per serving
‡ Less than 500 IU per serving
The international unit is the standard form of measurement for some nutrients, including vitamin A. For adult women, 1,000 IU represents 25 percent of the recommended daily allowance of vitamin A.

Vitamin A is a hardy element. Unlike some vitamins and minerals, it does not lose its strength over reasonable storage times or by cooking or in hot weather.

Vitamin A is produced as a supplement in many forms—pills, tablets, and powdered compounds. It is possible to get too much vitamin A, however; in terms of providing anti-cancer protection you should rely on foods to provide the carotene you need, which is not an overwhelming amount.

Most adults get half their daily vitamin A intake from fruits and vegetables; 25 percent from meat, poultry, or fish; 15 percent from milk, yogurt, cheese, and other dairy products; and about 10 percent from eggs and other foods. Some foods extremely high in vitamin A should be limited or avoided because they are also high in fat and calories—egg yolks, butter, whole milk and whole-milk cheeses, and liver.

PORTIONS THAT PROVIDE 1,000 IU OF VITAMIN A

Food	Portion
Acorn squash	
fresh, baked	¼
frozen	⅛
Apricot	
canned	2 halves
dried	2 large or 3 medium
Asparagus (green)	
canned	½ cup
fresh	8 medium spears
frozen	⅔ cup
Beans (green)	
fresh	1½ cups
frozen	1¼ cups
canned	1½ cups
Broccoli	
fresh	¼ cup
frozen	¼ cup
Brussels sprouts	
frozen	1 cup
Cantaloupe	¼ cup
Carrots	
raw	⅛ of 7-in. piece
canned	⅓ of 2-in. piece
Collards, frozen	1½ tbsp.
Green pepper	
raw	3 medium or 1½ large
Kale	⅛ cup
Mango	⅛ cup
Mustard greens	
fresh	⅛ cup
frozen	⅛ cup
Nectarine	
fresh	½
Papaya	
fresh	½ cup

Food	Portion
Peach	
fresh	1 medium or ½ large
canned	1 cup
Peas	
canned	1 cup
frozen	1 cup
Pumpkin	
canned	½ tbsp.
Romaine lettuce	1 cup
Spinach	
canned	1 tbsp.
frozen	1 tbsp.
raw	¼ cup
Summer squash (yellow)	
fresh	1½ cups
Sweet potato	
fresh, cooked	1 tbsp.
canned	1 piece, 1 in. in diameter and length
Tomato juice	½ cup
Tomatoes	
canned	½ cup
fresh	1
Turnip greens	
fresh	⅛ cup
frozen	⅛ cup
Mixed vegetables	
frozen	⅛ cup
Watermelon	
fresh	1 cup
Yellow corn	
canned	1⅓ cups
frozen	1¾ cups

VITAMIN C

Like carotene, vitamin C has also been identified as a cancer-protective element. This vitamin is thought to be able to reduce the risk of cancer of the stomach and esophagus; it may also work against development of bladder and colon cancer. Vitamin C may be most effective in blocking the formation of the harmful chemical nitrosamines in the stomach and intestines. Nitrosamines, which have been identified as carcinogens, are found in bacon after cooking, for example. But if a person eats or drinks a food rich in vitamin C before eating bacon, studies show that fewer or no nitrosamines are found in the digestive system.

Vitamin C also blocks another chemical reaction, oxidation. Many foods become spoiled or turn rancid if they are exposed to the air for too long; this reaction is oxidation. The anti-oxidation effect of vitamin C may protect the body from exposure to carcinogens in the atmosphere, in food, and in the workplace, scientists say.

Smokers, in particular, should increase their intake of vitamin C, because smoking lowers the amount of vitamin C in the bloodstream by 30 to 50 percent and increases the risk of oral and esophageal cancers.

Most of us are well acquainted with the sources of vitamin C. But the National Academy of Sciences has helpfully listed them:

VITAMIN C IN FOOD

Best Sources *	Moderate†	Low‡
Asparagus	Apricot	Apple
Broccoli	Banana	Celery
Brussels sprouts	Beet	Cucumber
Cabbage	Blackberries	Grapes
Cantaloupe	Carrot	Pear
Cauliflower	Cherries	Plum
Grapefruit	Corn	Pumpkin
Green pepper	Dark-green leafy vegetables	
Kohlrabi	Kale	
Lemon	Mango	
Lime	Peach	
Orange	Potato (white)	
Peas	Spinach	
Pineapple	Summer squash	
Raspberries	Watermelon	
Strawberries	Winter squash	
Sweet potato		
Tangerine		
Tomato		

Source: National Academy of Sciences Committee on Diet, Nutrition, and Cancer
* More than 20 mg. of vitamin C per serving
† 50 to 20 mg.
‡ Less than 5 mg.

The recommended daily allowance of vitamin C is 60 milligrams for adults. Since many fruits and vegetables rich in vitamin C are also good sources of vitamin A, it is often possible to combine the body's need for both in one serving of food. Some of these foods are:

Apricot	Mixed vegetables
Asparagus	Peach
Broccoli	Peas
Brussels sprouts	Romaine lettuce
Cantaloupe	Spinach
Corn	Sweet potato
Dark-green leafy vegetables	Tomato
Green beans	Watermelon
Green pepper	Winter squash
Mangoes	

Unlike vitamin A, however, vitamin C is highly perishable when exposed to heat, light, or oxygen; it cannot withstand long storage periods. The general rule is to buy these foods fresh and eat them as close to time of purchase as possible. It also helps to reduce the cooking time of these foods, steaming or stir-frying them rather than boiling them, or using limited water in boiling.

Vitamin C is believed to be nontoxic in all forms, including supplements in tablets, pills, and powders. For some people, there is no alternative to increasing the amount of vitamin C in their diet but taking a supplement. While it's always best to try to get all daily nutrients from food sources, there seems no medical evidence to argue against taking vitamin C in tablet or powdered form for most people. If, however, you are taking medication, especially dicumarol, tricyclic antidepressants, amphetamines, or warfarin sodium, or if you are pregnant, do not take vitamin C supplements without consulting your physician.

FIBER AND CANCER

After examining the medical research about the benefits of fruits and vegetables in the diet, it is not surprising to learn that the very structure of those foods also plays a positive role in staving off cancer. Fiber comes from the cell walls of plants; it is the material that provides their sturdy structure.

Dietary fiber is the component of food that cannot be broken down by enzymes in the human digestive tract; fiber apparently provides some protection from certain types of cancer—especially cancer of the colon and rectum, and some intestinal disorders—because it passes through the human digestive tract relatively intact. Most of fiber's bulk, however, acts like a sponge, absorbing large amounts of water from the intestines, binding to toxic and carcinogenic substances in the system, and carrying them out of the body as waste. Large amounts of fiber in the system remove substances from the stomach and intestines faster than if the foods—especially fats—were left to digest at their normal rates. Fiber, then, acts quickly to remove the substances that can cause cancer if they remain in the digestive tract.

FATS AND CANCER

The same high-fat diet associated with heart disease also increases the risk of developing certain cancers, including the leading life-threatening cancer—cancer of the colon—and cancer of the breast, the leading killer of American women. Cancer of the endometrium, the lining of the uterus, may also be related to a high quantity of fat in the diet. In some countries, including Japan, where the diet is low in fat and cholesterol, these cancers are uncommon.

Researchers have shown that when the diet contains abundant fats and cholesterol, bacteria that thrive in the stomach and digestive tract break down these foodstuffs into substances that can cause cancer directly or that promote the action of other cancer-causing chemicals. Fat itself is digested and emptied from the stomach more slowly than other substances in the diet. In addition, since high-fat diets contain relatively less of foods high in fiber, waste tends to remain longer than usual in the colon, exposing tissue to these carcinogens. The ultimate result, of course, is cancer.

Some substances produced from cholesterol by intestinal bacteria can mimic the action of female sex hormones and thus may promote the growth of cancer in hormone-sensitive tissues like the breast and endometrium. Increasing the risk of these cancers is another condition resulting from a high-fat diet: obesity. If you eat lots of fats, you are more likely to be obese than those whose diets are leaner. Obesity is another factor that increases the risk of developing cancers of the breast and endometrium.

Six

Preventing Premenstrual Syndrome

*P*remenstrual syndrome, or PMS, is a controversial condition whose very existence has been challenged by some who fear that the recognition of PMS in some way argues against equal rights for women. That's nonsense. Simply put, PMS is a common physiological problem, not a character defect. In most cases it can be eliminated or alleviated by changes in diet, by exercise, and by relaxation techniques.

Medical researchers say that most women—up to 85 percent of the menstruating female population—have experienced the symptoms identified with PMS in the days preceding their menstrual period, if only occasionally. About 40 percent of menstruating women, or approximately 27 million Americans, experience the symptoms regularly. For the vast majority of women, the symptoms of PMS are mild, involving complaints of irritability, bloating, fatigue, and headaches that merely signal the start of menstrual flow. For 5 to 10 percent of menstruating women, or about 3 to 7 million Americans, the condition is severe, marked by a range of physiological and psychological symptoms that disrupt their personal and professional lives.

While medical researchers still have many gaps to fill in their studies about PMS, this much is known:

PMS is a complex disorder apparently linked to the cyclic activity of the hypothalamic-pituitary-ovarian axis. The symptoms, which recur regularly at the same phase of each menstrual cycle and are followed by a symptom-free phase in each cycle, include depression, irritability, tension, headache, fatigue, breast swelling and tenderness, acne, asthma, abdominal bloating, weight gain, increased thirst or appetite, cravings for sweet or salty foods, and constipation. Other symptoms that may occur include boils, herpes, hives, epilepsy, migraines, dizziness, conjunctivitis, sties, uveitis, hoarseness, sore throat, sinusitis, rhinitis, cystitis, and urethritis. In extreme cases, the psychological and physical stress attributable to PMS has sometimes led to other problems, including alcohol abuse, panic attacks, psychotic episodes, suicide attempts, assaults, and child abuse.

Despite the lack of attention paid to the condition, the first research paper on PMS was actually published in 1931 by Dr. Robert Frank. Since then, more than 100 research studies on PMS and cyclic disorders related to menstruation have been published. Medical textbooks, however, continue to ignore or barely mention the syndrome and its symptoms. As a result, until recently, most physicians dismissed the complaint as a psychosomatic phenomenon or misdiagnosed it. Yet quite clearly, the condition exists; most women feel the changes in their body each month. While some women merely feel slightly uncomfortable or bloated premenstrually, others endure painful symptoms.

THE MENSTRUAL CYCLE

To understand PMS, you first have to understand the menstrual cycle.

Controlling a number of body systems, including the sex hormones, is the hypothalamus. Beginning with menarche and from each month thereafter until menopause, this walnut-sized unit buried deeply in the brain interprets the body's rhythms, transmitting messages to the pituitary gland that set the menstrual cycle in motion. In response, the pituitary produces two critical hormones: the follicle-stimulating hormone, known as FSH, and the luteinizing hormone, or LH. Once the hypothalamus signals the pituitary, the hypothalamus-pituitary-ovarian axis unites to prepare a woman's body for conception and child-bearing.

The monthly cycle is actually two phases, identified by the dominance of the hormone during each one: the follicular phase and the luteal phase. In the follicular phase, FSH is secreted into the bloodstream and reaches the ovary. FSH stimulates the development of the follicles of the ovary that contain egg cells. (Usually only one ovary and fifteen to twenty follicles are stimulated in a single cycle.) At the same time, the endometrium, or uterine lining, starts to develop and thicken in preparation for the potential implantation of a fertilized egg. The follicles start to develop, vying with each other for a dominant role. After the fifth day, a dominant follicle emerges and subsequently matures into an egg. The other follicles wither and die off, while FSH secretion stimulates the remaining follicle to manufacture estrogen, another sex hormone. On the eleventh and twelfth days of the cycle, a burst of estrogen is emitted, announcing to the pituitary that the follicle is about to produce an egg. The pituitary responds with a spurt of LH. This LH burst lasts for two or three days, overriding the influence of FSH and jolting the ovary into producing an egg. Within thirty-six hours, the ovary erupts with the egg.

Ovulation marks the beginning of the fourteen-day luteal phase. (The length of a menstrual cycle varies, but the luteal phase always lasts fourteen days. In the textbook example of a twenty-eight-day cycle, the follicular and luteal phases are both fourteen days. In a forty-day cycle, the luteal phase is fourteen days and the follicular phase is twenty-six days. Ovulation would occur on the last day of the follicular phase or the twenty-sixth day.) Then the egg leaves the ovary, passing through the Fallopian tubes to the uterus, available to be fertilized by male sperm. The follicle, now empty, changes character in response to the secretion of LH and becomes the corpus luteum, or yellow body. The corpus luteum manufactures and secretes hormones called progesterone and estrogen. The subsequent high concentration of estrogen in the bloodstream and pituitary inhibits the secretion of any more FSH or LH, which prevents them from signaling the ovary to develop any new follicles during this cycle.

If an egg is fertilized and a fetus conceived in the cycle, the corpus luteum flourishes. Enormous amounts of progesterone will be secreted to nurture and sustain the development of the fetus until the placenta takes over. Most cycles, however, do not result in pregnancy. In these cycles, then, the production of progesterone continues until a critical level is reached. When the pituitary detects that enough progesterone is in the bloodstream, it slows the production of LH. As LH production declines, the corpus luteum is no longer being fueled and it begins to decay. As the corpus luteum wanes, the amount of progesterone and estrogen being produced decreases. When the production of progesterone and estrogen bottom out, menstruation begins. The uterus is no longer stimulated by the hormones and the endometrium—the lining of the uterus—begins to slough off. After the first day or two of flow, the pituitary responds to the absence of estrogen and progesterone by making more FSH and preparing for the next cycle.

In some women, however, the delicate multi-system effort of the menstrual cycle is thrown out of balance. The result: the symptoms of PMS. Again, for most women—75 or 80 percent of us—these symptoms are simply mild but regularly experienced complaints that signal the onset of menstruation. Mild symptoms can almost always be eased by exercise and changes in diet, especially by eliminating salt, sugar, and caffeine.

The sex hormones—estrogen, progesterone, and the androgens (of which testosterone is dominant)—are all derived from cholesterol. They travel from the glands that secrete them through the blood to the target organs that utilize them. Hormones act upon their specific target organ by quickening the rate of internal cellular reactions. Estrogen and progesterone are believed to act as gene activators. Once inside the nucleus of the cell, the hormone activates the gene, initiating the synthesis of protein, and eventually influencing all of the functions of that cell.

Estrogen, secreted by the adrenal gland, is present in both males and females. In the female body it stimulates the development of breasts and the reproductive organs. In both sexes it acts on fat metabolism, and on the production of blood proteins and vascular and muscle tissue. The primary function of estrogen is in the menstrual cycle and the maintenance of the fetus. During the cycle, as follicles ripen in the ovary under the influence of FSH, they begin to secrete estrogen. The hormone travels back to the pituitary and there activates the surge in LH, which leads to ovulation. After ovulation the corpus luteum continues the follicle's job of producing estrogen, as well as progesterone. To facilitate the sperm's journey to the egg, estrogen also increases and thins out the cervical mucus, giving the sperm easier access to the uterus. Estrogen assists the egg's journey to the uterus by increasing the motility of the Fallopian tubes. It also nurtures the growth of the uterine endometrium that eventually anchors and feeds the fertilized egg.

In concert with the male hormone testosterone, estrogen halts bone development during adolescence by sealing the cartilage ends of the bones. A deficiency in estrogen leads to osteoporosis, a common disorder in postmenopausal women. Estrogen also accelerates the synthesis of the blood proteins and the metabolism of fatty acids that inhibit the production of cholesterol. It appears to protect women from heart disease and arteriosclerosis; the incident rates of heart disease among women are much lower than in men (but the rates increase in postmenopausal women). Estrogen also stimulates gland secretions in the skin—it helps maintain its elasticity and softness—and plays a role in normal vascular maintenance. As a result, estrogen deficiency, such as that experienced at menopause, may be marked by hot flashes.

Progesterone helps ready the endometrium for the implantation of a fertilized egg and sustains the fetus during pregnancy. Progesterone is estrogen-dependent; it requires prior stimulation by estrogen to do its work. Estrogen initially stimulates the growth of the endometrium, then progesterone steps in to convert the tissue into active glands. Under the influence of progesterone, the glands fill with glycogen to feed the fetus, blood vessels proliferate, and enzymes accumulate, ready to aid in the growth of the fetus. Like estrogen, progesterone is initially secreted by the ovary's corpus luteum, later by the placenta. One of its functions is to prevent another egg from being fertilized once one is in place in the uterus. After fertilization, it causes the cervical mucus to become thick and sticky, which locks sperm out and further protects the fertilized egg and uterus from bacteria. Progesterone also elevates the body temperature slightly, which is why we can determine the time of ovulation and peak fertility by tracking a woman's temperature.

In men, the principal sex hormone is testosterone, secreted by the testes. It is responsible for the production of sperm, the development and maintenance of male reproductive organs, and secondary sex characteristics such as pubic hair, deepened voice, coarser skin texture, thicker secretion of oil by the skin glands, and male muscle and fat distribution. It accounts for sex drive and growth—in both men and women; the adrenal glands produce small amounts of testosterone in women. This hormone may also account for the greater aggressiveness of males.

What does this all mean? The cyclical pattern of sex hormone activity and the changes of hormone supply between one cycle of life and the next produce physical, emotional, and behavioral changes.

In some women, these changes are accompanied by observable shifts in mood and health on a monthly basis; in others, visible changes are never apparent or are not apparent every month.

To those who insist that recognizing PMS will set back the women's movement, it is important to emphasize that men also are subject to cyclical hormonal surges and accompanying behavioral or psychological changes. In men, however, these shifts are often attributed to "moodiness." The ebb and flow of male hormones are not as dramatic as those in women but they are observable. In some men a stretch of good-neutral-bad temper occurs at regular intervals—thirty days, forty days, fifty-five days, or so—that are observed by family, friends, and co-workers, who adapt their own behavior toward and expectations of the men to account for the mood swings. In 1970, Danish researchers reported on sixteen years of data they had collected that showed that men experience a definite thirty-day cycle of testosterone production. In 1969, a study funded by the Omi Railway Company of Japan reported that male workers had predictable cycles that affected their work efficiency, decision making, and proneness to accidents. In reponse, the railroad revised its work schedules, removing employees from critical duties during their "bad" or unpredictable phases. At the University of Minnesota, Dr. Franz Halberg is conducting research into cyclical behavior in males. His early data showed evidence of cyclical surges and declines in grip strength and beard growth due to changes in hormonal levels. Given the hormonal changes in both sexes, it appears that equal rights exist even in that area.

Before PMS can be treated, it must be identified. Since its symptoms encompass so many systems of the body, it can be difficult to diagnose. But there are several signs that one can look for:

- PMS tends to begin at puberty, after pregnancy, after discontinuance of the birth-control pill, or after an episode of amenorrhea (no periods).
- Mild symptoms may be present for years but are suddenly—and surprisingly—increased after any of the following: discontinuance of the birth-control pill, a pregnancy, termination of breast-feeding, a tubal ligation or hysterectomy, or an episode of amenorrhea.
- Pelvic discomfort or pain may occasionally be a part of PMS, but painful menstruation is not. Painful menstrual cramps may be a symptom of dysmenorrhea or pelvic inflammatory disease. Some

women do find that changes in diet ease the pain of cramps—especially the elimination of salt, refined sugar, and caffeine.

- Many women with PMS experience monthly weight swings of 6 to 9 pounds, and over the years experience weight ranges of 28 pounds or more.
- Hunger and eating binges, especially involving sweet or salty foods, are often noted in the premenstrual phase. Some women report that acute symptoms, including violent episodes, panic attacks, and migraine headaches, often occur after an absence of food intake exceeding four or five hours.
- Women suffering from PMS may notice a decreased tolerance for alcohol premenstrually, accompanied by alcohol cravings.
- Some women experience weight gain, depression, headaches, and worsening of other symptoms if they use birth-control pills.
- Some women with a history of postpartum depression have PMS. (The depression must have been of sufficient severity to require psychiatric treatment or admission to a hospital.) One study of women admitted to hospitals for severe PMS found that 73 percent of those who had been pregnant had suffered from significant postpartum depression.
- A history of threatened abortion and other problems in pregnancy, especially hypertension or toxemia, may also be a PMS symptom. Bleeding in the early months of a pregnancy followed by a successful pregnancy is relatively common in PMS cases.
- Women with PMS may experience an increase in libido, or sex drive, during the premenstrual phase. On the other hand, women suffering from PMS as well as depression may experience a decreased interest in sex.

Before deciding whether or not you suffer from PMS, there's another checklist to review, for PMS is commonly misdiagnosed. Among the conditions it has been mistaken for are:

Dysmenorrhea—pelvic pain or menstrual cramping, generally beginning one day prior to the onset of menstruation and ending during or with the end of the flow.

Endometriosis—a painful condition marked by severe cramps and heavy bleeding that results when endometrial tissue (the lining of the uterus) appears and proliferates outside of the uterus, clinging to the ovaries, uterine ligaments, vagina, vulva, cervix, intestines, or pelvic lymph glands. In rare cases endometriosis may spread to the kidneys, lungs, arms, hands, thighs, or spleen.

Pelvic Inflammatory Disease—an umbrella term for various types of infections of the uterus, Fallopian tubes, ovaries and adjacent tissues, marked by severe pelvic and abdominal pain or abdominal swelling, nausea, vomiting, and high fever.

AN END TO PMS

Now that the medical community has acknowledged that PMS exists and its symptoms are not psychosomatic, treatments for it have also been identified. Research shows that most women can eliminate or ease their monthly symptoms by modifying their diet, getting more exercise, and using relaxation techniques to reduce stress. In most cases, this will erase or control the monthly complaints adequately. Women who have severe forms of PMS may need to consult physicians who specialize in its treatment with other therapies, but they too will likely be urged to change their diet as part of their treatment.

Many women with PMS are overweight; in some cases, this is a result of their repeated monthly cravings for sweet or salty foods. From studies of PMS sufferers, a dietary profile of the typical woman with PMS has emerged: she eats more refined carbohydrates, refined sugars, dairy products, and sodium, and less zinc, B vitamins, magnesium, manganese, and iron than a woman without PMS. Many women with PMS have food disorders: binge eating is the most common problem, and anorexia and bulimia have also been reported. (See chapter 8.)

Few women with PMS suffer from a condition known as hypoglycemia, but many PMS sufferers share some of the symptoms of hypoglycemia (see chapter 7). In the week before menstruation, the female body is more responsive to insulin; refined sugar increases the ability of insulin to act on the system. Many women have low blood-sugar levels in their premenstrual phase, and the ingestion of refined sugar during that time can have devastating effects on them psychologically and physically. Some women grow faint, teary, irritable, or depressed if they eat refined sugar. Stress can also lower blood-sugar levels; caffeine and nicotine exacerbate the problem, and thus should be avoided.

Women who experience fluid retention—swelling of the face, hands, feet, or breasts, or weight gain in the days preceding their periods—as part of their premenstrual symptoms should try to eliminate salt from their diet, especially prior to menstruation. Studies of women suffering from fluid retention have shown that they have elevated levels of hormones of the adrenal glands, which control water and salt retention by the kidneys. These salt-retaining hormones are stimulated when stress and high brain serotonin trigger the release of a brain hormone called ACTH. Excess refined carbohydrates increase brain serotonin. Insulin also plays a role. Excess refined carbohydrates trigger insulin release in excess. Insulin is known to prevent the kidneys from excreting salt. Salt and water retention is in part an insulin effect. For many women with PMS, the craving for sweets and subsequent ingestion of large amounts of refined carbohydrates or sugar precede the swelling and weight gain, which seems to confirm the roles of refined sugar–triggered insulin release. Poor nutrition decreases resistance to stress. Stress by itself causes the adrenal glands to release in the blood increased amounts of salt-retaining hormones, which increases the salt-retaining effect of insulin.

Women with PMS should restrict their intake of sugar, sodium, caffeine, dairy products, and red meat, and increase the amount of complex carbohydrates and foods high in B vitamins, magnesium, calcium, and other essential nutrients. These recommendations are the same many nutrition experts offer to anyone who wants to improve his or her health and diet. Some physicians suggest that PMS sufferers, like hypoglycemics and diabetics, divide their daily calorie intake into six eating times a day: three meals a day with a midmorning snack, a midafternoon snack, and a snack before bedtime.

The following prescription will ease or eliminate the symptoms of PMS in most women:

1. Restricting red meat to less than 3 ounces a day. Limit total protein intake to 4 ounces a day on a 1,000-calorie diet or 7 ounces of protein on a 1,500-calorie diet. The best sources of protein are fish, poultry, whole grains, and legumes.

2. Limiting dairy products—eggs, cheese, milk, yogurt, butter—to 2 servings a day. Protein from all sources—meat, fish, leg-

umes, and dairy products—should represent no more than 20 percent of total daily calories.

3. Increasing complex carbohydrates—vegetables (especially green leafy vegetables), fruits, whole grains—to 50 to 65 percent of total daily calories, the higher the better.

4. Reducing refined sugar intake to, ideally, 5 teaspoons a day. Eliminate candy, chocolate, cake, pie, pastries, and ice cream from your diet. If you must have something sweet, eat fresh fruit.

5. Limiting fats from all sources to 20 percent of total calories each day.

6. Reducing salt intake to less than 3 grams a day. Soft drinks, club soda, and tonic water—even diet sodas—have large amounts of salt in the form of sodium benzoate. Drink seltzer, mineral water, or plain tap water on ice instead.

7. Reducing or eliminating caffeine (coffee, tea, cola drinks, chocolate). Use decaffeinated coffee or tea. Caffeine increases the body's need for B vitamins. Caffeine makes breast symptoms—breast swelling, engorgement, and tenderness—worse and may increase irritability, hyperactivity, and headaches.

8. Limiting alcohol intake to 1 ounce of hard liquor a day, 4 ounces of wine, 12 ounces of beer.

9. Using safflower oil in cooking and salad dressings; it contains cis-linoleic acid, which is believed to alleviate some of the symptoms of PMS.

10. Avoiding processed and fast foods, which contain large amounts of salt, sugar, and chemicals.

A dramatic change in diet and elimination of all "bad" foods from the diet may be difficult for many women for long periods of time. But the results for PMS sufferers can be dramatic. The best way to carry through the PMS prescription probably is to start gradually: by reducing caffeine, salt, sugar, alcohol, and red meat; and by increasing vegetables, whole grains, cereals, and fruits. After a few weeks, try to reduce the intake of the "bad" foods even more and increase the healthy ones. See if you don't feel better. Almost everybody does.

The PMS diet is only one of several changes you should make to ease monthly symptoms. Increase the amount of exercise you get and try to reduce stress in your life. Yes, it will take a lot of effort. But it will be worth it.

Seven

The Hypoglycemia Story

*W*ith fast-food restaurants dotting the landscape from coast to coast and processed and heavily sugared and salted foods filling our supermarket shelves, it is no surprise that 20 to 40 million Americans suffer from a nutritional and endocrine imbalance stemming from overdoses of sugar. Hypoglycemia affects more women than men, especially women between thirty and forty years of age.

Hypoglycemia is a metabolic disorder. Normally, the body takes all sugars introduced into its system and changes them into glucose, or blood sugar. Hypoglycemia—literally, low blood sugar—is a condition of faulty glucose metabolism in which an increased production of insulin drains the body of glucose. Because every cell of the body requires glucose to function, the resulting glucose starvation can play havoc with all the body's systems.

Normally, following a meal, there is an immediate rise in the blood-sugar level, as carbohydrates, including refined sugar, are rapidly metabolized and absorbed into the bloodstream. This escalating level of glucose triggers the production of insulin, a hormone secreted by the pancreas. Insulin removes much of the glucose and stores it in the liver in the form of glycogen for later use as fuel for the body. In the hypoglycemic, however, the pancreas runs amok, producing too much insulin, which rapidly drains the blood of its glucose supply. Blood-sugar levels plummet rapidly and the body becomes starved for food, despite the fact that it has recently been fed.

Most cells in the body can store some glucose. The brain cannot; it depends on a continual supply from the bloodstream. If the brain becomes starved for glucose, it will grow exhausted and malfunction. A healthy diet provides intermittent supplies of carbohydrates, protein, and fat throughout the day—that's why nutritionists usually recommend that people eat three balanced meals daily. The regulation of the body's glucose is controlled by the hypothalamus and involves hormonal secretions, the nervous system, and dietary intake. When the body's sensors indicate to the hypothalamus that a low-blood-sugar condition—hypoglycemia—exists, this complex system reacts to increase glucose levels in the blood and reduces the amount of glucose sent to the brain and peripheral cells, including the muscles. This readjustment of the body's balance of glucose triggers symptoms of hypoglycemia, including faintness, weakness, tremulousness, blurred vision, hunger, palpitations, fast pulse rate, sweating, tightness in the throat, restlessness, irritability, and even anxiety. If the brain is deprived of glucose for a sufficient length of time, other symptoms may occur, including depression, headache, forgetfulness, confusion, lack of coordination, and eventually seizures and coma. The hypoglycemic episode ends when enough glucose is released from the liver or when the individual obtains enough glucose from food.

Hypoglycemia is a relative condition. Some individuals diagnosed as hypoglycemic may have low blood-sugar levels that, when measured, fall within the normal range. Yet their bodies perceive the level to be abnormal and unnecessarily produce large amounts of insulin and epinephrine (adrenaline).

The disorder is identified by a glucose-tolerance test, which monitors the body's sugar metabolism over several hours—after fasting and after ingesting a large amount of carbohydrates and sugars. Flattened glucose-tolerance curves indicate an increased tolerance for sugar. Obesity is a frequent complication, because the hypoglycemic is often hungry. In recent years, some researchers have suggested a high rate of hypoglycemia among the obese, hyperkinetic children, schizophrenics, alcoholics, drug addicts, and juvenile delinquents.

Caffeine, nicotine, and stress exacerbate the hypoglycemic response. Caffeine and nicotine are powerful stimulants that along with stressful situations cause the body to manufacture adrenaline, which in turn triggers the production of insulin. One way the body reacts to stress is by lowering blood-sugar levels. This, in turn, triggers a craving for refined sugar—some women may want only chocolate—that is fulfilled by an eating binge. Stress, then, like PMS, is one culprit in the binge-eating cycle. As a result, the hypoglycemic may wind up feeling exhausted, hungry, depressed, anxious, and tense. If a lot of refined sugar is then consumed, the effects can be debilitating. Highly refined sugar forces an amino acid into the brain cells, where it is converted to serotonin. Too much serotonin may cause nervous tension, palpitations, and drowsiness. Combine stress with a high intake of refined sugar, and you set in motion a self-perpetuating, debilitating cycle.

Refined sugar triggers insulin release in excess of what is needed. Refined sugar also increases the ability of insulin to act by three to eleven times. In the premenstrual period, when blood-sugar levels are likely to be lower than usual, ingesting refined sugar can trigger mood swings, depression, crying jags, fainting spells, and other problems.

Hypoglycemia can be treated with a proper diet designed to stabilize the blood-sugar level, which is why the hypoglycemic should eat several small meals or snacks several times a day rather than one or two or three large meals. Sugar is absorbed into the bloodstream faster than any other food. Complex carbohydrates, especially whole grains, nuts, and vegetables, are also converted to glucose after ingestion, but at a slower rate. Proteins and fats are metabolized more slowly as well; consequently the blood sugar rises much more slowly and consistently. The classic hypoglycemic diet, therefore, substitutes proteins and fats for most of the sugar in a diet. But don't try to treat yourself. Consult your physician and take a glucose-tolerance test, if you think you might have hypoglycemia.

Eight

Out of Control: Eating Disorders

*T*he typical American doesn't eat well; she eats a great deal of the wrong things as far as nutritional value is concerned. In our pressure-filled, affluent society, food has been transformed from one of life's necessities to an element that many have chosen to overdose on. Instead of using food for its essential nutrients, we may turn to food for basic pleasure and comfort—as a reliable and comforting friend when we are bored, angry, lonely, sad, or frustrated. Our culture reinforces that tendency. Television commercials and super-market aisles offer a parade of sugared cereals, ice cream, puddings, cakes, pies, and candy, alongside cartons of heavily salted, sugared, floured, and chemically processed foods that can be prepared instantly.

This environment is a mine field for many. Researchers know that depression and obesity may be due in part to an over-release of certain chemicals that act on the brain's hunger response, distorting an individual's response to and perception of food, and sometimes triggering cravings. Depression and food cravings recur regularly in many women. This may be a result of a hormonal imbalance in the body.

Binge eating—the sudden, compulsive ingestion of very large amounts of food in a very short time, sometimes furtive, sometimes public—is usually triggered by stress or by feelings of loneliness, frustration, anxiety, tension, or boredom, or is a symptom of an un-derlying emotional illness, such as depression. It is extremely com-

67

mon among women, a significant percentage of whom are also depressed. Dr. Hilde Bruch, in her book *Eating Disorders,* writes, ". . . eating binges, uncontrolled eating in response to the slightest insult or disappointment, have occurred at some time or another in practically all" of her patients. And the binges are almost always followed by self-recrimination.

Food binges wreak havoc in the lives of millions of women who can't control their cravings for or attitudes toward food. Bruch observes that for many bingeing has an important positive function; it is a compensatory mechanism in a frustrating and stressful life. In others, however, it is associated with, and directly related to, severe personality and developmental disturbances. Many people, she says, hide their emotional problems "under a complacent facade. . . . Instead of expressing anger, or even experiencing it, they become depressed and the overeating serves as a defense against deeper depression. . . . Overeating may occur at times of such severe emotional stress that the question is not so much 'Why overeating?' but 'What would be the alternative?' "

Statistics show that obese people have a higher incidence of most diseases and a higher death rate, but their suicide rate is dramatically lower. There's a correlation, according to Bruch. Some people become obese in reaction to emotional problems and crises in their lives, situations in which she says "others might have reacted with despair. However much of a handicap obesity may become, as a defensive reaction it is less destructive than suicide or paralyzing deep depression."

Cravings for food—and especially for chocolate, sweets, or salty foods—are experienced frequently and sometimes monthly by some women during their premenstrual phase. When the cravings are strong, they result in binge eating. Women who eat compulsively may be incapable of stopping themselves. When women of normal weight and normal eating patterns binge briefly, they usually lose the extra 4 or 5 pounds immediately afterward; women who suffer from PMS and who binge may lose the weight once their period begins. Some women gain 8 to 15 pounds by bingeing and eventually have great difficulty losing this weight afterward. (Of the women with PMS who are overweight, at least 75 to 80 percent binge, and about 20 percent are more than 25 pounds overweight.)

Links between food cravings and menstruation, and food cravings and depression, have been studied by many scientific researchers. Stuart Smith and Cynthia Sauder studied 300 nurses and did a pilot study of 37 hospitalized depressive patients. They found that of the group of depressed patients, 15 women, or more than 40 percent, said they felt like eating compulsively prior to menstruation. Nine of those 15 women, or 24 percent, reported experiencing premenstrual depression. Of 16 of the 37 patients who also said they craved sweets, 12 patients, or 75 percent, said they suffered from premenstrual depression. All 9 patients who said they craved chocolate had premenstrual depression.

Sixty-six percent of the 300 nurses studied said they were tense or depressed just before or at the start of their periods. The nurses' study also showed "a rather striking association between recurrent depression, premenstrual fluid retention, and a peculiar craving for sweets in the immediate predepressive and premenstrual period." Of the 116 who reported a desire to eat compulsively at specific times, 85, or 73 percent, said they had premenstrual tension or depression. Of the 64 who said they craved sweets at specific times, 49, or 77 percent, said they had premenstrual tension or depression. Of the 42 who craved chocolate at specific times, 34, or 81 percent, reported premenstrual tension or depression. Smith and Sauder began the study after their observation of 3 depressed female patients "who demonstrated a peculiar and characteristic craving for sweets" before their periods that was "not present under normal circumstances. These persons did not normally tend to eat compulsively nor were they obese. Just prior to a period of depression, however, they reported a very powerful craving for sweets and in particular for chocolate, which they went to great lengths to obtain."

Another study of 45 women, including 25 with premenstrual symptoms, reported irritability, fatigue, depression, crying spells, impatience, and craving for sweets. Still another researcher, Joseph Morton, reported an alteration in carbohydrate metabolism to permit increased sugar tolerance. "The hypoglycemia is a recent and striking finding in premenstrual tension. It is clinically manifested by increased appetite or a craving for sweets." In Morton's study, 37 percent of the women with PMS had cravings for sweets and 23 percent had increased appetite. Tests of the women with premenstrual tension showed that they were hypoglycemic prior to the onset of their periods.

ANOREXIA NERVOSA AND BULIMIA

Younger women—usually adolescents but sometimes women in their twenties—sometimes have a reverse eating disorder called anorexia nervosa. Anorexics usually start by dieting from a slightly overweight or normal level with a goal of 10 or more pounds under what would be an ideal weight. When they reach that level, though, they keep on dieting, refusing meals, balking at their favorite foods, until their weight plunges to 90, 80, sometimes 70 pounds or less. Estimates of the incidence of anorexia range from 1 in 100 adolescent girls to 1 in 200.

Bulimia is a disorder that occurs in a wide range of women—from schoolgirls to women in their thirties or forties—who maintain their ideal weight through a bizarre pattern of bingeing and purging. Their external appearance is usually completely normal. But their private lives can be hellish struggles to gain control over their eating habits. Such well-known women as Jane Fonda and Jill Clayburgh have admitted to having experienced bulimia in their early careers, when any extra weight would have jeopardized their popularity and yet their private anxieties and depression caused them to turn toward food for release. Experts say it is impossible to estimate the incidence of bulimia because there are no outward symptoms.

Women trapped by these conditions have a distorted view of their own self-image and of food itself. Anorexics, for example, suffer from an underlying "disturbance of delusional proportions in the body image and body concept," according to Dr. Bruch. The anorexic seems to be completely unaware of her actual weight and size, insisting to her parents and friends that she is fat, when she is actually little more than a walking skeleton. Some anorexics pursue thinness as part of their struggle for an independent identity, their preoccupation with food, and their striving for perfection. It is the ultimate, self-selected malady for a teenager unable to confront her emerging maturity. Anorexic girls frequently come from extremely close families and are "the perfect" daughters who earn high grades in school and are usually very obedient. Anorexia is usually their only form of rebellion. Very recently, the problems of these eating disorders have come to be diagnosed and treated widely. Many women who binge occasionally or even once a month may find that they can bring their cravings under control by following the diet guidelines and recipes in this book. We hope so. Others may find themselves locked into a cycle of bingeing and starving or bingeing and purging; they should seek medical or psychological attention to help them resolve their problem.

Nine

Menopause and Osteoporosis

*T*he onset of menopause signals the end to a woman's fertility, what Anne Sexton called the "November of the body." This harsh reality is at least partly absorbed by the length of the process; menopause spans three to seven years for many women. Menopause used to occur around age forty, but women now are more likely to experience it at fifty or fifty-one. Women's longer reproductive life, with earlier puberty and menarche and delayed menopause, has evolved with improvements in nutrition and health care.

The physical signs of menopause, however, may still start in the forties as the menstrual cycle gradually decreases in length. At fifteen, the average cycle is thirty-five days; at twenty-five, it is thirty days; at thirty-five, twenty-eight days. Between forty and fifty, the cycle often shortens to twenty-one days. Then some cycles are missed, some are shorter, some are longer. The extreme irregularity of the cycles can be confusing and frustrating; usually the cycles have a clearcut beginning but an uncertain end. The irregular bleeding is the result of stimulation of the remaining follicles, which in turn secrete estrogen.

As estrogen levels drop, the remaining follicles increasingly fail to muster the strength to reach ovulation. Without ovulation there is no corpus luteum, no secretion of estrogen and progesterone, no noticeable growth of the endometrium, and no bleeding. The decrease in estrogen takes a toll on the organs that have been nurtured by that hormone. The female reproductive organs wither. Without estrogen the vagina may begin to atrophy and excrete a brownish discharge, as its capillaries break down and rupture. The secretion of mucus also dwindles. The uterus begins to shrink because the endometrium is no longer being stimulated by the follicles. Slowly the transition from normal menstruation to permanent amenorrhea is completed: no longer is each month marked with a flow of blood.

Depression, irritability, crying spells, and flaring temper may accompany the onset of menopause. Estrogen-replacement therapy may alleviate some of the psychological problems associated with menopause. Some women also experience hot flashes, which also can be eased by estrogen therapy. The flashes may last only a second or as long as ten minutes; they can be frequent, unsettling, manifested by a sudden sensation of heat or burning, followed by intense perspiration. Usually the flash begins with the sensation of a mild headache or cranial pressure. This quickly mounts to a burning hot spell that spreads through the upper body with a resulting red flush. Often the flash will permeate the entire body in short, quick waves and the woman's temperature will rise for a moment until the sweating appears, restoring the temperature to normal. Hot flashes may also trigger fatigue, weakness, and dizziness. The mechanism causing the flashes is still unknown.

The most serious health hazard of menopause is osteoporosis, a skeletal disorder where the bones begin to lose mass and strength, becoming brittle and easily broken. This is why the body shrinks with age. Osteoporosis is more common in women than in men; ovarian malfunction is one factor, but the cause of this degenerative disorder remains unknown. Everyone loses bone strength with age, partly due to loss of calcium. But an estrogen deficiency compounds the problem. Short-term estrogen therapy may help halt the process of bone degeneration and calcium loss.

Osteoporosis can be caused by a diet deficient in calcium and vitamin D. The gradual loss of bone minerals that occurs in osteoporosis can be inhibited, halted, or reversed by adequate calcium and vitamin D supplements.

Osteoporosis is an insidious disease; the symptoms are usually not apparent until the disease is in the advanced stages. In many cases, the progressive weakening of the bones, as porous gaps develop where minerals are removed, first shows up when bones of the hip, spine, or limbs simply break spontaneously. In some women, especially those who are postmenopausal, low-back pain is the first symptom. Loss of bone mass in the spine eventually results in shortening of height and "dowager's hump."

Current estimates are that more than 14 million women are visibly affected by osteoporosis in the United States. That is not to say that men and other women are not affected in some way. We all lose minerals from our bones. The difference is that men start losing bone density between the ages of forty-five and fifty-five, while in women the process starts about ten years earlier. In the United States, more than one-third of the more than a million fractures that occur in women over forty-five every year are associated with osteoporosis. Other studies have found a close correlation between bone density and hip, vertebral, and long-limb fractures in women. Osteoporosis severe enough to cause fractures is estimated to occur in at least 10 percent of men and women over fifty.

Orthopedists explain, however, that the fractures are not actually caused by the falls that frequently are cited as their cause. First, the doctors say, the bones become thin and brittle; typically the hip joint becomes so fragile that it snaps or breaks *and then* the person falls. Such hip fractures occur about eight times as frequently in women as in men, due to progressive estrogen loss as well as lack of calcium.

The first bone where demineralization usually occurs is the jaw. When tooth-bearing bone is lost, the result is periodontal disease. Like osteoporosis, periodontal disease is insidious. It begins at a relatively early age and progresses many years before teeth are loosened and finally lost. Almost 80 percent of Americans have some degree of periodontal disease, and fully half have lost teeth to the disease by the age of sixty. Periodontal disease, of course, involves many symptoms besides loss of minerals from the jaw bone. Nevertheless, progressive loss of alveolar (jaw) bone and detachment of teeth have been associated with calcium deficiency or imbalance and osteoporosis in other areas of the body.

Eliminating the calcium deficiency can inhibit or possibly reverse the loss of bone density. Studies undertaken at Cornell Medical College and the University of Göteborg, Sweden, involved giving 500-milligram supplements of calcium (in the form of calcium gluconolactate and calcium carbonate) twice a day to 10 people with periodontal disease. The daily diet was found to contain only 200 to 350 milligrams of calcium in 9 of the 10 people (1 person had a daily intake of 850 milligrams). After six months of supplementation, symptoms such as bleeding gums, gingivitis, and loose teeth either disappeared or were remarkably reduced. Bone loss was stopped, and in 7 out of 10 people was reversed: bone density increased in the tooth-bearing bone.

Another group of researchers confirmed that low dietary calcium levels led to resorption of alveolar bone, and went on to test the effects of daily supplements of 750 milligram of calcium (calcium carbonate) plus vitamin D (375 IU) on people who had already lost teeth because of bone demineralization. Bone density was not increased in this trial, but loss of density was reduced by 34 to 39 percent.

Calcium supplements apparently can also strengthen other bones as well. In studies at the Burke Rehabilitation Center in White Plains, New York, 12 elderly women between the ages of seventy-nine and eighty-nine were given supplements of 750 milligram of calcium plus 375 IU of vitamin D. After three years of supplementation, the average bone density of the group increased by 6 percent. In a matched group of women who did not take supplements, bone density decreased by 7 percent. Physicians at Burke then tried calcium supplements on a group of younger women, aged thirty-six to sixty-two. No changes in bone density were measured during the first six to nine months. After that, however, changes started to occur, dramatically in some women, slowly and steadily in others. After three years of supplementation, bone density in 6 (out of 14) women rose to the level found in men of similar ages. One of the women stopped taking supplements, and within a year her bone density fell from well above the normal level for her age to below normal.

Many doctors maintain that the reason women start to lose bone density is the reduction in hormone levels that begins around the time of menopause. This is a controversial point, because women are known to lose bone density even before estrogen levels start to drop. Nevertheless, the standard treatment for menopausal osteoporosis in many doctor's offices is still estrogen supplements.

The Burke researchers also conducted a study in which the effects of calcium supplements were compared to the effects of estrogen supplements. One group of women received calcium alone; one received calcium plus estrogen; one received estrogen alone; and one received placebo pills. The women who received calcium alone or calcium with estrogen did experience increased bone density. But the women who received a placebo or estrogen alone continued to lose bone density. In a later study of bone density and fracture risk in women who were taking estrogen supplements, it was found that calcium intake, more than estrogen, was the predicting factor in bone density and fracture risk.

Studies by other researchers have confirmed these successes in halting or reversing loss of bone density because of inadequate calcium in the diet.

Another factor involved in osteoporosis—one which no amount of supplementation can replace—is exercise. Bone loss occurs in both men and women whenever exercise or physical activity is severely reduced. Even the astronauts were found to lose bone density during space flights when exercise programs were insufficient. It doesn't require extended periods of inactivity to cause bone loss, because the astronauts started losing significant amounts of calcium after only three days. One study demonstrated that as little as one hour of exercise three times a week resulted in an increase in bone density in 18 postmenopausal women.

A study of the biochemical effects of exercise helped explain this phenomenon by showing that exercise increased blood levels of calcium and affected certain hormone levels in such a way as to favor maintenance of bone density. Other studies have shown that skeletal mass is usually higher in runners. And finally, one study revealed that even among men and women of college age (twenty to twenty-five), variations in bone density were associated with levels of physical activity and the amount of calcium in the diet. Even young adults, then, can reduce their chances of developing osteoporosis later in life. Women of all ages should make sure they have enough calcium in their diets and enough physical activity in their lives.

Ten

In Motion

*R*egular exercise is as important as a balanced diet to maintaining good health; it is also as difficult for some people to maintain an exercise regime as a diet that permits no sweets or butter. Yet the nation is on the move, with more than 30 million joggers and runners, 5 to 10 million aerobic dancers, and devoted hordes of tennis and squash players, bicyclists, and golfers. No matter what form you prefer, it's important to get yourself in motion and stay there.

For weight control alone, exercise can play a critical role. After all, you have to either eliminate 3,500 calories from your diet or burn up a similar amount in exercise in order to lose a single pound. Most Americans are at least 10 or more pounds overweight. Thirty-five thousand calories! That's a lot of food deprivation. Or a healthy amount of exercise, balanced with reduced calorie intake. And which way is the easier way to lose?

The following chart shows just how energetic you have to be to work off the calories of even healthy foods, like apples.

EXERCISING YOUR WAY THIN

Food	Calories	Walking	Biking	Jogging	Swimming
		(minutes to burn off calories listed)			
Apple (1 medium)	87	17	11	9	8
Bacon (2 slices)	96	19	12	10	9

Food	Calories	Walking	Biking	Jogging	Swimming
		(minutes to burn off calories listed)			
Banana (1 medium)	127	24	16	13	11
Beans (½ cup, cooked, green)	15	3	2	2	1
Beer (8 oz.)	115	22	14	12	10
Bread and butter (1 slice)	96	18	12	10	9
Carrot, raw (1 large)	42	8	5	4	4
Cereal, dry (1 cup with milk and sugar)	212	41	26	21	19
Cheese, American (1-oz. slice)	112	22	14	11	10
Cheese, cottage (1 rounded tbsp.)	30	6	4	3	3
Chicken, fried (½ breast)	232	45	28	23	21
Cookie, vanilla wafer (1 average)	15	3	2	2	2
Cookie, chocolate chip (1 average)	50	10	6	5	5
Egg, boiled or poached (1 medium)	78	15	10	8	7
Egg, fried or scrambled (1 medium)	108	21	13	11	10
French dressing (1 tbsp.)	57	11	7	6	5

Food	Calories	Walking	Biking	Jogging	Swimming
		(minutes to burn off calories listed)			
Halibut, broiled (1 serving)	214	41	26	21	19
Ham, fresh, cooked (2 slices)	254	49	31	25	23
Ice cream (⅔ cup)	186	36	23	19	17
Ice milk (⅔ cup)	137	26	17	14	12
Mayonnaise (1 tbsp.)	100	19	12	10	9
Milk, skim (8 oz.)	88	17	11	9	8
Milk, whole (8 oz.)	160	36	20	16	14
Milk shake (8 oz.)	420	81	51	42	38
Orange (1 medium)	73	14	9	7	7
Orange juice (4 oz.)	54	10	7	5	5
Pancake (1 with 2 tbsp. syrup)	204	39	25	20	18
Peach (1 medium)	38	7	5	4	3
Peas (½ cup cooked)	58	11	7	6	5
Pizza (⅛ of 14-in. cheese pie)	185	36	23	19	17
Potato chips (5 2-in. chips)	54	10	7	5	5
Sherbet, orange (⅔ cup)	120	23	15	12	11
Shrimp, fried (3½ oz.)	225	43	27	23	20
Spaghetti, w/meat sauce (1 serving)	396	76	48	40	35

Food	Calories	Walking	Biking	Jogging	Swimming
		(minutes to burn off calories listed)			
Steak (8 oz.)	235	45	29	24	21
Tuna sandwich	278	54	34	28	25

Exercise, especially aerobic exercise, is strongly recommended by physicians and the American Heart Association as an essential part of a program to prevent heart disease.

Osteoporosis is another condition that can be prevented by exercise. A study done by researchers at the University of North Carolina showed that athletic women aged fifty-five to seventy-five had the bone density of much younger women, and had bones 15 to 20 percent denser than those of sedentary women the same age. Especially valuable are exercises that involve work against gravity, such as walking, jogging, cycling, and tennis. Swimming, though it provides excellent muscle-toning opportunities and may be a great aid in weight control, is of little use in increasing bone density, according to the university study.

Exercise has also been seen to ameliorate the symptoms of depression, anxiety, fatigue, irritability, nervous energy, premenstrual headaches, and cramps. Depression is especially helped by regular exercise; studies have shown that the improvement in the efficiency of the cardiovascular and respiratory systems caused by aerobic exercise speeds recovery from depression, increasing the flow of oxygen to the brain. Many women who embark on a regular exercise program also report a lessening of the severity of their PMS symptoms.

Why does exercise help? It speeds up weight loss on any type of diet. It improves circulatory and oxygenating capacity. It may also increase the secretion of progesterone and beta-endorphins, the hormones that are released by the brain and produce a sensation of mild euphoria.

Physicians say that a regular exercise routine requires three sessions a week for a minimum of twenty minutes each time. Fifteen minutes of vigorous exercise are required to boost your heart rate and increase its efficiency. No more than two days should elapse between workouts, or the gains made on Wednesday will be lost by Friday night.

If you start a regimen, remember that exercise should stretch and flex your muscles, not cause pain. If you feel pain, stop. Aches and stiffness, however, are the natural byproducts of a new exercise regime. A long soak in a hot tub, sauna, or Jacuzzi will turn that stiffness into a memory.

The amount of body fat rather than muscle mass you have is one way to determine if you're in good condition. Try the pinch test for body fat. Extend your arm away from your body so that the upper arm is level with your shoulder and bend your elbow slightly to make a muscle. With the thunb and forefinger of the other hand, pinch the skin on the back of the raised arm over your triceps muscle in the middle of your under-upper-arm. The pinch should be made lengthwise. Estimate the amount of skin and fat you can pinch, or have a friend measure it with a ruler. The average amount of skin and fat a physically fit person has is one-half to three-quarters of an inch. If you have less than one-quarter inch of skin and fat, you have a very low body-fat level and are probably in better-than-average shape. If you pinch more than three-quarters of an inch, you've got a lot of work to do to get in shape.

Aerobic exercises, which increase cardiopulmonary fitness, should be part of any program. They will increase cardiovascular and respiratory efficiency and strength, and flexibility of the large muscles of the body. The best aerobic exercises are bicycling, swimming, jogging, running, and aerobic dancing.

An aerobic program should help you reach a "target zone" of 60 to 80 percent of your maximum attainable pulse rate. Generally, this maximum attainable rate is determined by subtracting your age from the number 220. Sixty to 80 percent of that figure is your target zone. (If you're thirty years old, your target zone is 114 to 152 beats a minute, or 60 to 80 percent of 190.)

To test yourself, pause at intervals during your workout and take your pulse. In taking your pulse at your wrist, never use the thumb because it has a pulse of its own. Instead, use the second and third fingers, placing them along the inside, or thumb side, of your wrist. Press in gently until you feel the beat of the artery. Looking at the second hand of a clock or watch, count the beats in a ten-second time period and multiply by 6 to determine the rate per minute. An alternative method is to take the pulse of the artery in your neck. Again using the second and third fingers, gently probe down from the jaw bone and push in lightly until you feel the pulse beat. Again, count the beats in a ten-second period and multiple by 6.

For aerobics beginners, the pulse rate should be kept toward the lower limit of the target zone, so the heart isn't overtaxed. As your body condition improves and the cardiorespiratory system strengthens, you should try to approach the upper limit.

Any aerobic regimen should include:

- A five-to-ten-minute warm-up and moderate aerobic exercises to stimulate the circulatory system and warm up the muscles
- A ten-to-twenty-minute peak period, in which you reach and maintain your target-zone pulse rate
- A five-to-ten-minute cool-down routine of moderate aerobic exercises that permits the blood to return to all parts of the body and not remain trapped in the hands or feet

Whatever method of exercise you choose, it should be one that gives you good health and a good attitude. While it may be a struggle to start, you should find that the benefits to be gained will soon make you look forward to your exercise sessions week in and week out.

Introduction to the Recipes

Thanks to the growing movement toward lighter cuisine, dieting no longer has to mean deprivation. Most women (and men) want to eat well but soundly, yet few have time to spend most of the day in the kitchen. For this reason, in developing these recipes we tried to create gourmet meals that would be relatively easy to prepare.

For the sake of simplicity, I often use the same ingredients in the recipes, such as safflower oil and Fontina cheese. As you will know from the text, safflower oil is one of the best vegetable oils (especially for women), although you may certainly substitute any other vegetable oil. The same goes for the Fontina; I happen to like its nutty flavor, but you should feel free to use any low-fat cheese.

Most of these recipes call for fresh ingredients. This, of course, may not be possible in certain seasons or in certain parts of the country, even though many fine fresh ingredients are now available year-round. Tomatoes are one exception, certainly; often in the winter I will use canned tomatoes instead of fresh (allowing two canned tomatoes for one fresh). You can equally well use plum tomatoes, which are much more flavorful off-season than the other tomatoes that are available. And while fresh produce is always preferable, you may want to substitute canned tomatoes at times when you don't want to bother with skinning and seeding the fruit.

The nutritional information has been calculated from the United States Department of Agriculture's handbook *Nutritive Value of American Foods*. All amounts are figured for one serving.

Where there are two suggestions for a particular ingredient (water-cress or sorrel, for example), the first one figures in the calculations; optional ingredients and garnishes have not been included.

Bon appetit.

—LIS BENSLEY
November 1985

Eleven

Soups

FRESH TOMATO SOUP

This delightful soup is best made with fresh tomatoes. If good summer tomatoes are not available, however, low-sodium canned plum tomatoes can easily be substituted.

2¼ pounds tomatoes
1 tablespoon safflower oil
3 shallots
4 cloves garlic, minced
4 tablespoons tomato paste
3½ cups Chicken Broth (page 87), or canned low-sodium broth
4 tablespoons chopped fresh basil, or 2 teaspoons dried
¼ teaspoon thyme
1 bay leaf
Pepper to taste

Bring a large saucepan of water to a boil. Put in a few tomatoes at a time, boil for 30 seconds, remove, and cool under cold running water. This allows the skins to slide off easily. Cut the tomatoes in half widthwise and, holding a tomato half in your hand, gently squeeze out the seeds. Drain on paper towels, then chop.

In a large saucepan, heat the oil and sauté the shallots, stirring frequently, until soft. Add the garlic and chopped tomatoes, lower the heat, and simmer for 5 minutes. Stir in the tomato paste, then the broth and herbs. Cover the pan and simmer for 30 minutes. Purée the soup in a food processor or blender, and season to taste with pepper. *Serves 4.*

Calories: 172.2   Calcium: 68.5 mg.
Protein: 7.8 g.   Iron: 4.1 mg.
Fat: 4 g.   Sodium: 138.5 mg.
Carbohydrates: 22.6 g.   Potassium: 991.6 mg.
                           Vitamin A: 3,560.7 IU
                           Vitamin C: 78.1 mg.

CHICKEN BROTH

Because commercial chicken broth is laden with sodium, it's a good idea to make your own. It is easy and inexpensive to prepare and will keep for several days in the refrigerator or for several months in the freezer.

        1 pound chicken bones, or a chicken carcass
        2 carrots, chopped
        1 leek, white part only, chopped
        1 onion, quartered
    4-5 peppercorns
      ¼ teaspoon thyme
    4-5 parsley sprigs
        1 bay leaf
        8 cups water

Put the bones or the carcass in a large soup pot with water to cover. Simmer the bones for 2 minutes, pour off the water, and rinse off the bones. Return the bones to the pot with the remaining ingredients. Let the water come to a boil, then lower the heat and simmer, covered, for 1 hour. Strain the broth through a strainer or cheesecloth and chill until the fat congeals on the surface. Skim off the fat before using. *Makes 8 cups.*

Per 1-cup serving: Calcium 12.5 mg.
Calories: 45 (approx.) Iron: 1.3 mg.
Protein: 3.5 g.   Sodium: 129 mg. (approx.)
Fat: trace   Potassium: 0
Carbohydrates: trace Vitamin A: 0
Vitamin C: 0

CREAM OF WATERCRESS
OR SORREL SOUP

Sorrel is not always easy to find but is well worth looking for. It makes an excitingly delicate soup, although watercress is a fine substitute. Both watercress and spinach are rich sources of calcium and vitamin C.

> 3 cups watercress or sorrel leaves, tightly packed
> 1 cup spinach leaves, tightly packed
> 1 tablespoon safflower oil
> 4 scallions, sliced
> 3½ cups Chicken Broth (page 87), or canned low-sodium
>   broth
> 2 tablespoons fresh lemon juice

Wash the watercress or sorrel and spinach leaves well, then dry on paper towels.

Heat the oil in a large saucepan. And the scallions and cook until they are soft. Add the greens and cook, stirring constantly, until they are wilted.

Stir in the broth, bring to a boil, then reduce the heat and simmer for 5 minutes. Purée the soup in a food processor or blender. Return the soup to the pan, stir in the lemon juice, reheat, and serve. *Serves 4.*

Calories: 86.3   Calcium: 44.6 mg.
Protein: 4.1 g.   Iron: 1.7 mg.
Fat: 3.6 g.   Sodium: 121.5 mg.
Carbohydrates: 4.1 g. Potassium: 178.4 mg.
                      Vitamin A: 3,120.1 IU
                      Vitamin C: 17.1 mg.

BROCCOLI SOUP

This soup is adapted from a recipe of my grandmother's. It is delicious hot and makes a perfect summer lunch when served cold with a salad. Among vegetables, broccoli is a nutritional gold mine: it is high in calcium, iron, potassium, vitamins A and C, and fiber. And it is low in calories, fat, and sodium.

  1 tablespoon safflower oil
  1 small yellow onion, chopped
  1 stalk celery, sliced
  1 small leek, trimmed of green top, well washed, and thinly sliced
  1 clove garlic, minced
  6 cups Chicken Broth (page 87), or canned low-sodium broth
  1 bunch broccoli
    Low-fat yogurt (optional)

Heat the oil in a large saucepan and sauté the onion, celery, and leek until wilted. Stir in the garlic and the chicken broth.

Chop the broccoli into small pieces. Separate the stems from the flowerets. Add the stems to the broth and bring the liquid to a boil. Reduce the heat, cover, and simmer for 10 minutes. Add the flowerets, cover, and simmer another 10 minutes.

Purée the soup in a food processor or blender. Serve warm with a dollop of low-fat yogurt, if desired, or serve cold. *Serves 6, generously.*

Calories: 109.8   Calcium: 95.5 mg.
Protein: 6.7 g.   Sodium: 149.7 mg.
Fat: 2.5 g.   Iron: 2.3 mg.
Carbohydrates: 9.2 g.   Potassium: 422.5 mg.
                         Vitamin A: 1,513 IU
                         Vitamin C: 74.2 mg.

CARROT SOUP WITH CURRY

This soup has a sweet flavor with a pungent aftertaste. It is easy to make and is excellent cold as well as hot; it has enough body to make a good light meal with a salad. Carrots, of course, are loaded with vitamin A and are a good source of fiber.

>   4 cups Chicken Broth (page 87), or canned low-sodium
>   broth
>   4 carrots, peeled and sliced
>   1 small Granny Smith apple, peeled, cored, and chopped
>   ½ medium onion, chopped
>   1–2 teaspoons curry powder, to taste
>   ½ teaspoon turmeric
>   Low-fat yogurt (optional)

Heat the broth in a large saucepan. Add the remaining ingredients. Bring the liquid to a boil, then lower the heat. Cover and simmer for 30 minutes.

Purée the mixture in a food processor or blender. Thin the soup, if necessary, with a little more chicken broth. Serve warm or cold with a dollop of low-fat yogurt, if desired. *Serves 4, generously.*

Calories: 129.7   Calcium: 71.8 mg.
Protein: 5.4 g.   Iron: 2.3 mg.
Fat: 0.6 g.   Sodium: 179.2 mg.
Carbohydrates: 19.7 g. Potassium: 390.6 mg.
                         Vitamin A: 15,780 IU
                         Vitamin C: 13.3 mg.

CAULIFLOWER SOUP WITH DILL

Cauliflower and dill make a surprisingly good combination. This soup is simply prepared and is especially good if made a day before serving. Cauliflower is a good source of vitamin C, and the leeks are high in calcium.

½ head cauliflower
4 cups Chicken Broth (page 87), or canned low-sodium broth
1 leek, trimmed of green top and well washed
2 tablespoons finely chopped fresh dill, or 1 teaspoon dried

Chop the cauliflower into small pieces, reserving a few small flowerets for garnish, if desired.

Heat the broth in a large saucepan. Add the cauliflower and leek and bring the liquid to a boil. Reduce the heat, cover, and simmer for 30 minutes.

Purée the soup in a food processor or blender. Thin the soup, if desired, with a little more chicken broth. Stir in the dill, garnish with reserved flowerets, and serve warm or cold. *Serves 4, generously.*

Calories: 70.4   Calcium: 40.7 mg.
Protein: 4.1 g.   Iron: 2.1 mg.
Fat: 0.2 g.   Sodium: 135.3 mg.
Carbohydrates: 5.2 g.   Potassium: 216.6 mg.
                        Vitamin A: 225.1 IU
                        Vitamin C: 32.3 mg.

FRESH PEA AND SPINACH SOUP

Mint gives this soup a sweet, refreshing flavor. Use fresh peas, if you can; canned or frozen peas are a poor substitute. The spinach lends this recipe an iron and vitamin A boost.

      1 pound peas
      1 tablespoon safflower oil
      4 scallions, thinly sliced
      4 cups Chicken Broth (page 87), or canned low-sodium
        broth
      ½ pound spinach leaves, well washed
      2 tablespoons fresh mint, finely chopped, or ½ teaspoon
        dried
        Low-fat yogurt (optional)

Shell the peas.

Heat the oil in a large saucepan and sauté the scallions until wilted. Add the broth, the peas, and the reserved pods. Bring the liquid to a boil, reduce the heat, and simmer, covered, for 15 minutes.

Stir in the spinach leaves and simmer until wilted, about 3 to 4 minutes. Purée the soup in a food processor or blender. Return the soup to the saucepan, stir in the mint, and reheat. Serve with a dollop of low-fat yogurt, if desired. *Serves 5.*

      Calories: 106.8   Calcium: 69.4 mg.
      Protein: 6.6 g.   Iron: 3.2 mg.
      Fat: 3.0 g.   Sodium: 137.4 mg.
      Carbohydrates: 8.2 g. Potassium: 361.8 mg.
                             Vitamin A: 3,048.6 IU
                             Vitamin C: 38.4 mg.

ONION SOUP

This is one of the easiest, most flavorful, and least expensive soups. The longer you sauté the onions before adding the broth, the sweeter their flavor will be. You can, of course, always top the soup with a thick, toasted slice of whole wheat French bread and some grated part-skim cheese, such as Jarlsberg or Fontina, and melt the cheese under the broiler.

      1 large onion (about ¾ pound), halved and thinly sliced
   1½ tablespoons safflower oil
      4 cups Chicken Broth (page 87), or canned low-sodium
         broth
      ½ cup white wine
      1 bay leaf
      1 teaspoon freshly ground pepper

Sauté the onion in the oil over low heat, stirring frequently, until it is very tender, about 10 to 15 minutes. Add the chicken broth, wine, bay leaf, and pepper. Let the liquid come to a boil, then lower the heat and simmer, covered, for 1 hour. Remove the bay leaf before serving. *Serves 5.*

Calories: 112.5   Calcium: 28.5 mg.
Protein: 3.7 g.   Iron: 1.3 mg.
Fat: 4.1 g.   Sodium: 17.2 mg.
Carbohydrates: 6.2 g.   Potassium: 115.6 mg.
                         Vitamin A: 24 IU
                         Vitamin C: 6.3 mg.

LENTIL SOUP

This flavorful and hearty soup makes a good winter supper with a salad and a whole wheat baguette. The lentils are high in protein, calcium, and potassium and the carrots provide generous amounts of vitamin A and fiber.

                1 onion, quartered
                2 carrots, chopped
                1 stalk celery, chopped
                1 leek, white part, chopped
             4½ cups Chicken Broth (page 87), or canned low-sodium
                   broth
                3 shallots, chopped
                2 cloves garlic, crushed
              ½ teaspoon thyme
              ¼ teaspoon marjoram
                1 bay leaf
                3 tablespoons lemon juice
              ½ cup lentils
                   Pepper to taste
                3 carrots, chopped
                1 tablespoon chopped fresh parsley

Mix all ingredients except the chopped carrots and parsley in a large saucepan. Bring the liquid to a boil, reduce the heat, and simmer, covered, for 1 hour.

Purée the soup in a food processor or blender, and return to the saucepan. Add the carrots and simmer for 10 to 15 minutes, until the carrots are tender. Serve, sprinkled with parsley. *Serves 6.*

Calories: 128.1   Calcium: 87.2 mg.
Protein: 6.5 g.   Iron: 2.7 mg.
Fat: 1.9 g.   Sodium: 153.6 mg.
Carbohydrates: 20.7 g.   Potassium: 850 mg.
                           Vitamin A: 13,361 IU
                           Vitamin C: 21 mg.

WINTER VEGETABLE SOUP

A hearty soup that's made with winter vegetables, this can be served as a meal with a green salad.

    ½ onion, finely chopped
    1 leek, white part, chopped
    1 stalk celery, chopped
    1 carrot, chopped
    1 white turnip, chopped
    2 cloves garlic, minced
    8 cups Chicken Broth (page 87), or canned low-sodium
        broth
    1 bay leaf
    ½ teaspoon oregano
    1 cup cooked white beans
    ¼ cabbage, shredded
    1 cup spinach leaves
        Pepper to taste
        Finely chopped parsley for garnish

In a large saucepan, combine the onion, leek, celery, carrot, turnip, and garlic with the broth and herbs. Bring the liquid to a boil, then lower the heat and simmer, covered, for 30 minutes.

Add the beans, cabbage, and spinach and simmer another 10 minutes. Season to taste with pepper, and garnish with a little chopped parsley. *Serves 4.*

Calories: 209.4   Calcium: 127.8 mg.
Protein: 13.6 g.   Iron: 5.2 mg.
Fat: 0.6 g.   Sodium: 317.7 mg.
Carbohydrates: 23.7 g. Potassium: 676.3 mg.
                        Vitamin A: 4,838.7 IU
                        Vitamin C: 35.8 mg.

GAZPACHO

One of my favorite summer soups, this gazpacho is a pungent adaptation of the classic Spanish recipe. It is a rich source of calcium, potassium, and vitamins A and C.

> 6 tomatoes, peeled, seeded, and chopped (see page 85), or
>   1 32-ounce can low-sodium tomatoes, well drained
> 1 small onion, chopped
> ½ green pepper, seeded and chopped
> ½ cucumber, peeled, seeded, and chopped
> 1½ cups tomato juice, preferably low-sodium
> 2 cloves garlic, minced
> 1 teaspoon cumin
> 1 teaspoon pepper
> 2 tablespoons olive oil
> 3 tablespoons wine vinegar
>   Finely chopped onion, green pepper, and cucumber for garnish

Purée the tomatoes, onion, green pepper, and cucumber in a food processor or blender. Add the tomato juice, garlic, cumin, and pepper, and process to blend.

Pour the soup into a bowl, cover, and chill at least 3 hours. When ready to serve, stir in the oil and vinegar, and garnish with chopped vegetables. *Serves 6.*

Calories: 113.7	Calcium: 44.2 mg.
Protein: 3.4 g.	Iron: 1.6 mg.
Fat: 5.1 g.	Sodium: 64 mg.
Carbohydrates: 15.9 g.	Potassium: 674.6 g.
	Vitamin A: 1,572.5 IU
	Vitamin C: 75.6 mg.

COLD CUCUMBER-LEEK SOUP

1½ pounds cucumber
 1 leek, white part only, chopped
 4 cups Chicken Broth (page 87), or canned low-sodium broth
 ½ cup low-fat yogurt
 2 tablespoons chopped fresh dill
    Pepper to taste
    Chopped chives for garnish

Peel the cucumber, cut out the seeds, and chop. In a large saucepan, mix the cucumber with the leek and the broth. Bring the broth to a boil, lower the heat, and simmer, uncovered, for 20 minutes.

Purée the soup in a food processor or blender. Stir in the yogurt and dill. Season to taste with pepper, and chill until ready to serve. Serve garnished with chopped chives. *Serves 4.*

Calories: 92.5   Calcium: 86.9 mg.
Protein: 5.9 g.   Iron: 2.1 mg.
Fat: 0.7 g.   Sodium: 153.3 mg.
Carbohydrates: 8.9 g.   Potassium: 357.5 mg.
                        Vitamin A: 224.1 IU
                        Vitamin C: 23.1 mg.

Twelve

Salads

TOMATO, CUCUMBER, RED ONION, AND BASIL SALAD

Use fresh summer tomatoes and basil, if you can, for this salad, which is the perfect complement to most fish dishes.

   2 tomatoes, sliced
   ½ cucumber, peeled and sliced
   ¼ red onion, thinly sliced
   ½ cup Simple Vinaigrette (page 224)
   3 tablespoons fresh basil, chopped, or 1½ teaspoons dried

On 4 salad plates or a large platter lay a row first of tomatoes, then of cucumber, then of red onion. Spoon a little vinaigrette over all, and sprinkle with chopped basil. *Serves 4.*

Calories: 133   Calcium: 42.5 mg.
Protein: 2.2 g.   Iron: 1.5 mg.
Fat: 10.4 g.   Sodium: 32.1 mg.
Carbohydrates: 9.6 g. Potassium: 400.7 mg.
                       Vitamin A: 1,082.3 IU
                       Vitamin C: 36.9 mg.

TOSSED GREENS
WITH ANCHOVY-LEMON DRESSING

    1 bunch watercress
    1 bunch arugula
    1 garlic clove, crushed
    1 head green- or red-leaf lettuce, or romaine
  6–7 fresh basil leaves, if available, chopped

DRESSING:
½–1 teaspoon anchovy paste, to taste
    2 tablespoons lemon juice
    1 tablespoon olive oil
    2 tablespoons safflower oil
      Freshly ground pepper to taste

Cut the ends off the watercress and arugula. Rub a large wooden salad bowl with the garlic, then toss in the greens. Add the anchovy paste, lemon juice, and oils, and toss until well mixed. Season to taste with pepper, adding more anchovy paste, if necessary. *Serves 6.*

Calories: 80.6   Calcium: 47.3 mg.
Protein: 1.7 g.   Iron: 0.8 mg.
Fat: 7.3 g.   Sodium: 6.8 mg.
Carbohydrates: 2.9 g.   Potassium: 217.9 mg.
                        Vitamin A: 2,368.8 IU
                        Vitamin C: 22.5 mg.

BEET, WATERCRESS,
AND ENDIVE SALAD

2–3 beets (about 1 pound)
   4 cups watercress, tightly packed
   2 endives
   ½ cup Lemon-Mustard Dressing (page 226)

Cut the greens and the ends off the beets. Cook them in a pot of boiling water until they are tender, about 30 to 45 minutes, depending on their size. Drain, cool under cold running water, and peel off the outer skin. Slice the beets and let them cool until ready to use.

On 4 salad plates, arrange a bed of watercress. Top the watercress with the beet slices. Separate the endives into leaves and lay them on the sides of the beets. Drizzle with the dressing. *Serves 4.*

Calories: 207.2
Protein: 3.2 g.
Fat: 17.3 g.
Carbohydrates: 12 g.

Calcium: 84.1 mg.
Iron: 1.8 mg.
Sodium: 151.9 mg.
Potassium: 571 mg.
Vitamin A: 4,747.7 IU
Vitamin C: 30.3 mg.

GUACAMOLE

Although relatively high in calories, avocadoes are also loaded with potassium and vitamins A, C, and E. Yogurt makes this guacamole lighter and especially tasty; it also increases the calcium and thins out the calories.

        2 ripe avocados (about 1½ pounds)
       ¼ onion, chopped
        1 jalapeño pepper, seeded and chopped
     1½ tablespoons lemon juice
        1 clove garlic
       ¼ teaspoon cumin
       ½ teaspoon coriander
       ¾ cup low-fat yogurt
        1 tomato, peeled, seeded, and chopped (see page 85)

In a food processor, purée the avocados, onion, jalapeño pepper, lemon juice, and garlic until smooth. Add the cumin and coriander and process just to mix. Scrape the guacamole into a bowl. (You can also mash the avocado in a bowl with a fork, then stir in the remaining ingredients.)

Stir in the yogurt, and chill. Before serving, mix in the chopped tomatoes. Serve on a bed of lettuce with sliced vegetables, if desired. Or use as a topping on enchiladas. *Serves 6.*

Calories: 150.9   Calcium: 58.1 mg.
Protein: 3.1 g.   Iron: 0.7 mg.
Fat: 12.7 g.   Sodium: 19.6 mg.
Carbohydrates: 12.3 g.   Potassium: 645.6 mg.
                         Vitamin A: 472.4 IU
                         Vitamin C: 26.2 mg.

ORIENTAL SALAD

Once the stuff of esoteric Oriental gourmands, tofu has become a staple of today's fat-conscious society. And it's an excellent source of calcium and iron. Because of its bland taste, tofu lends itself to a variety of flavorings and can be added to many dishes, such as this salad. If you are restricting your salt intake, use light soy sauce.

½ head cauliflower
½ pound broccoli
½ pound mushrooms, sliced
 4 scallions, thinly sliced
½ cucumber, peeled and sliced
 1 red pepper, seeded and cut into strips
2–3 tomatoes (about 1 pound), cut into wedges
 2 (8-ounce) cakes tofu
    Lettuce leaves
¼ pound bean sprouts

DRESSING:
 1 cup cider vinegar
½ cup safflower oil
 2 tablespoons sesame oil
 2 tablespoons soy sauce
 1 tablespoon sesame seeds
 1 garlic clove, minced
 1 tablespoon fresh ginger, grated

Separate the cauliflower and broccoli into flowerets. Combine all the vegetables except the lettuce and bean sprouts in a large bowl. Cut the tofu into 1-inch cubes and add the vegetables.

Whisk the dressing ingredients together until well mixed and pour over the vegetables. Toss gently to not break up the tofu. Serve the salad on a bed of lettuce, topped with bean sprouts. *Serves 7.*

Calories: 278.2   Calcium: 160.5 mg.
Protein: 9.8 g.   Iron: 3.4 mg.
Fat: 21.1 g.   Sodium: 441.3 mg.
Carbohydrates: 29.4 g.   Potassium: 579.4 mg.
                         Vitamin A: 2,247.9 IU
                         Vitamin C: 104.5 mg.

TABOULI

1 cup fine bulgur wheat
3 cups water
2 tomatoes, peeled, seeded, and chopped (see page 85)
3 scallions, finely chopped
¾ cup chopped fresh parsley
4 tablespoons lemon juice
1 tablespoon safflower oil
1 tablespoon olive oil
3 tablespoons fresh chopped mint, or 1 teaspoon dried
　Pepper to taste
　Lettuce leaves
　Sliced cucumbers

Soak the bulgur in the water for 30 minutes, until soft. Drain through a colander lined with a towel, squeezing out any excess water.

In a large bowl, mix the remaining ingredients. Let sit for at least 30 minutes before serving. Serve on a bed of lettuce with sliced cucumbers, if desired. *Serves 4.*

Calories: 227.2　　　Calcium: 86.8 mg.
Protein: 9.5 g.　　　Iron: 3.8 mg.
Fat: 8.8 g.　　　　　Sodium: 41.4 mg.
Carbohydrates: 29 g.　Potassium: 608.9 mg.
　　　　　　　　　　Vitamin A: 1,275 IU
　　　　　　　　　　Vitamin C: 39.4 mg.

TOMATO ASPIC

Often, I fill a ring mold of tomato aspic with cottage cheese, chicken salad, or tuna salad for lunch. It is also good with a vinaigrette or Dill Sauce (page 216).

4 cups low-sodium tomato juice or V-8
1 tablespoon horseradish
2 tablespoons Worcestershire
3 tablespoons lemon juice
2 cloves garlic, minced
2 envelopes gelatin

In a large saucepan, mix the tomato juice or V-8, horseradish, Worcestershire, lemon juice, and garlic, and bring to a boil. Lower the heat and simmer for 10 minutes. Remove the pan from the heat and stir in the gelatin until well mixed. (There should be no lumps.)

Pour the tomato mixture into a ring mold, cover with plastic wrap, and refrigerate overnight. Just before serving, dip the mold into a large pan of hot water, then invert it onto a platter. Decorate the aspic with greens, drizzle with dressing, or fill with chicken or seafood salad or cottage cheese, if desired. *Serves 4.*

Calories: 67.6	Calcium: 19.6 mg.
Protein: 6 g.	Iron: 1.9 mg.
Fat: 0.2 g.	Sodium: 139.7 mg.
Carbohydrates: 10.4 g.	Potassium: 494.6 mg.
	Vitamin A: 1,600.2 IU
	Vitamin C: 35.6 mg.

EGG SALAD

Try this old standby in vegetable cases or tomato cups (see page 209).

    4 eggs
    2 tablespoons mayonnaise
    ¼ teaspoon dry mustard
      Pepper to taste

Poke a hole in the large end of each egg with a pin. (This allows the air inside to escape so that the shells do not crack while cooking.) Cook the eggs at a slow boil in a large saucepan for 10 to 12 minutes. Drain and refill the pot with cold water. Crack the shells and let the eggs sit in the cold water until they have cooled. Peel the eggs, cut 2 in half, and discard their yolks.

Chop the eggs, and add the remaining ingredients. Chill until ready to serve. Serve in tomato cups, on a bed of greens garnished with tomato slices, or as sandwiches in pita bread. *Serves 2.*

Calories: 250.8   Calcium: 36 mg.
Protein: 10.7 g.   Iron: 1.4 mg.
Fat: 22.4 g.   Sodium: 169.9 mg.
Carbohydrates: 1.1 g.   Potassium: 119.5 mg.
                         Vitamin A: 705 IU
                         Vitamin C: 0

CURRIED CHICKEN SALAD

        2 chicken breasts (about ¾ pound)
        1 stalk celery, finely chopped
        2 scallions, chopped
        1 peach, skinned and chopped
        1 mango, skinned and chopped
        ½ pound seedless green grapes, halved
       1½ ounces slivered almonds
       1¼ cups Curry-Yogurt Dressing (page 228)
          Lettuce leaves
          Fresh fruit slices

Poach and skin the chicken breasts, following the recipe on page 141. (Save the poaching liquid for chicken broth.) Chill until cool. Cut into bite-size pieces.

In a large bowl, mix the chicken with the celery, scallions, peach, mango, grapes, and almonds. Toss with the dressing, and serve on a bed of lettuce, garnished with fruit slices. *Serves 4.*

Calories: 293.9   Calcium: 124.5 mg.
Protein: 22.7 g.   Iron: 2.1 mg.
Fat: 8.7 g.   Sodium: 82.9 mg.
Carbohydrates: 35.9 g.   Potassium: 724.6 mg.
                         Vitamin A: 3,488.5 IU
                         Vitamin C: 29.5 mg.

DILL CHICKEN SALAD

Dill, mustard, and lemon combine to give this chicken salad an unusually refreshing taste. Use fresh dill if possible.

    3 chicken breasts
    ½ pound broccoli
    ¼ pound snow peas
    3 tablespoons cashews, toasted and coarsely chopped

DRESSING:
    ¾ cup low-fat yogurt
    3 tablespoons chopped fresh dill, or 1½ teaspoons dried
    1½ teaspoons Dijon mustard
    2 tablespoons lemon juice
    ½ teaspoon pepper

Poach the chicken breasts, following the recipe on page 141, and cool. Cut the chicken into bite-size pieces and reserve.

Discard the stems from the broccoli and separate the flowerets. Cut the stems off the snow peas. Steam the broccoli until it just begins to feel tender, then add the snow peas and steam another minute. Remove the vegetables immediately and cool.

To make the dressing, mix the yogurt, dill, mustard, lemon juice, and pepper in a bowl. In another large bowl, mix the chicken, broccoli, snow peas, and cashews. Add the dressing and toss until well blended. Serve on a bed of greens. *Serves 4.*

Calories: 228.9
Protein: 29.7 g.
Fat: 7.6 g.
Carbohydrates: 11.5 g.

Calcium: 144.8 mg.
Iron: 2.4 mg.
Sodium: 226.1 mg.
Potassium: 664.3 mg.
Vitamin A: 1,660.7 IU
Vitamin C: 64.2 mg.

LENTIL SALAD

¾ cup lentils
1 zucchini, diced
2 carrots, diced
1 Granny Smith apple, cored and chopped
4 scallions, chopped
½ cup chopped fresh parsley
¼ cup raisins

DRESSING:
¼ cup fresh lemon juice
2–3 teaspoons curry powder, to taste
⅓ cup safflower oil

Rinse the lentils well and put them in a saucepan with 3 cups of water. Let the water come to a boil, then lower the heat and simmer, covered, until the lentils are tender, about 30 minutes. Add more water if too much evaporates. While the lentils are cooking, chop the vegetables. Drain the lentils and chill until cool.

Just before serving, mix the lentils, apple, vegetables, parsley, and raisins in a large bowl. Make the dressing by whisking the lemon juice and curry powder together. Pour in the oil slowly, while whisking, until it is well mixed and slightly thick. Pour the dressing over the salad, toss well, and serve. *Serves 4.*

Calories: 260.4   Calcium: 67.1 mg.
Protein: 4.7 g.   Iron: 2 mg.
Fat: 15.5 g.   Sodium: 40.5 mg.
Carbohydrates: 28.5 g.   Potassium: 605.8 mg.
                           Vitamin A: 8,658.8 IU
                           Vitamin C: 31.1 mg.

SHRIMP AND WILD RICE SALAD

⅓ cup wild rice
¼ pound shrimp, peeled, cleaned, and deveined
¼ pound snow peas
4 scallions, sliced

DRESSING:
2 tablespoons safflower oil
1½ tablespoons lemon juice
1 tablespoon chopped fresh dill
¼ teaspoon dry mustard, or 1 teaspoon Dijon mustard

Rinse the wild rice well in a colander using cold water. Bring 1 cup water to a boil in a saucepan, stir in the rice, lower the heat, and simmer, covered, for 45 minutes, or until the rice is tender and the water is absorbed.

While the rice is cooking, bring 3 cups of water to a boil in a second saucepan, then lower the heat until the water simmers. Add the shrimp and cook until they just turn pink, about 3 to 5 minutes, depending upon their size. Drain immediately.

Remove the stems and strings from the snow peas. Steam them for a few minutes until they are just tender. Let the shrimp, rice, and snow peas cool before making the salad.

In a large bowl, combine the shrimp, rice, and snow peas with the scallions. In another bowl, whisk the dressing ingredients together and pour over the salad. Toss well, and serve on a bed of greens. *Serves 4.*

Calories: 153.4   Calcium: 40.1 mg.
Protein: 6.8 g.   Iron: 1.3 mg.
Fat: 7.1 g.   Sodium: 30 mg.
Carbohydrates: 16.7 g.   Potassium: 168.4 mg.
                         Vitamin A: 279.8 IU
                         Vitamin C: 11.5 mg.

TUNA AND PASTA
SALAD WITH HERBS

This salad is equally tasty without tuna, although less rich in iron and protein. If you have no problem with sodium, substitute 1 teaspoon Dijon mustard for the dry mustard.

        1 cup macaroni shells, preferably spinach or Buitoni Light
           (about 4 ounces)
        2 tomatoes, peeled, seeded, and chopped (see page 85)
        ½ pound green beans, sliced diagonally
        4 scallions, sliced
        1 red pepper, chopped into small chunks
        1 (3-ounce) can white tuna in water, drained
     1 ½ tablespoons chopped fresh basil, or 1 ½ teaspoons dried
        ½ teaspoon oregano
        1 clove garlic, minced
        3 tablespoons lemon juice
        ¼ teaspoon dry mustard
        1 tablespoon safflower oil
        1 tablespoon olive oil
          Pepper to taste

Cook the pasta until it is *al dente,* drain well, and allow to cool.
    In a large bowl, mix the pasta with the vegetables, tuna, basil, and oregano.
    In a small bowl, whisk the garlic, lemon juice, mustard, and oils. Pour the dressing over the salad and toss until well mixed. Season with pepper, and serve on a bed of lettuce. *Serves 4.*

Calories: 255.7   Calcium: 64.8 mg.
Protein: 12.5 g.   Iron: 6.5 mg.
Fat: 7.8 g.   Sodium: 9.8 mg.
Carbohydrates: 35.5 g.   Potassium: 493.5 mg.
                         Vitamin A: 3,209.4 IU
                         Vitamin C: 134.6 mg.

VEGETABLE AND WILD RICE SALAD

A grain indigenous to America, wild rice dates back to the early Indians of eastern Canada. Nutritionally, it is a perfect grain—higher in protein and lower in fat than most others. It is also a good source of B vitamins. Because of its nutritional value as well as its nutty taste and texture, wild rice is an excellent substitute for more traditional carbohydrate side dishes. It also is good cold as a salad.

⅓ cup wild rice
½ pound broccoli
½ pound green beans
¼ pound peas
¼ pound mushrooms
4 scallions
    Lettuce leaves
    Watercress sprigs

DRESSING:
½ cup low-fat yogurt
¼ teaspoon dry mustard
1½ tablespoons lemon juice
1 tablespoon chopped fresh basil, or ⅓ teaspoon dried
2 tablespoons chopped fresh parsley
    Fresh watercress for garnish (optional)

Rinse the wild rice in a colander. Bring 1 cup water to a boil, stir in the rice, and simmer, covered, for 45 minutes or until all the water is absorbed and the rice is tender. Let the rice cool before making the salad.

Separate the broccoli into flowerets. (Reserve the stems for soup.) Dice the beans. In a large pot, steam the broccoli, beans, and peas until just tender, about 5 minutes. Let cool.

Slice the mushrooms and the scallions.

In a large bowl, combine the rice with the vegetables. In another bowl, whisk the dressing ingredients together well, pour over the salad, and toss quickly but thoroughly. Serve on a bed of lettuce and garnish with sprigs of watercress, if desired. *Serves 4.*

Calories: 122.3   Calcium: 126.9 mg.
Protein: 7.3 g.   Iron: 2.2 mg.
Fat: 1 g.   Sodium: 31.8 mg.
Carbohydrates: 23.4 g.   Potassium: 568.9 mg.
                         Vitamin A: 1,783.1 IU
                         Vitamin C: 72.9 mg.

FRUIT SALAD WITH TOFU-ORANGE DRESSING

Tofu is a fine substitute for mayonnaise; it is not only lower in calories and fat, but also higher in protein, iron, and calcium, and its flavor is more subtle. This salad is perfect for a summer lunch, and can be made with whatever combination of fruits you like.

   2 peaches, cored, pitted, and sliced
   1 pint strawberries, halved
   1 pint blueberries
   ¾ pound seedless green grapes, halved, or 3 kiwis, peeled and sliced
   ½ cantaloupe, scooped into balls
   3 tablespoons chopped fresh mint

DRESSING:
   1 (8-ounce) cake tofu
   ½ cup water
   3 tablespoons frozen orange juice concentrate
   1 tablespoon honey

Combine the fruit in a large bowl, and add the mint.

In a blender, combine the dressing ingredients and purée until smooth. Serve the fruit on a bed of greens, topped with a dollop of dressing. *Serves 4.*

Calories: 208.7   Calcium: 112.5 mg.
Protein: 8.8 g.   Iron: 3.2 mg.
Fat: 2.8 g.   Sodium: 16.5 mg.
Carbohydrates: 44.9 g.   Potassium: 585 mg.
                         Vitamin A: 3,422.3 IU
                         Vitamin C: 99.6 mg.

Thirteen

Egg and Cheese Dishes

SPINACH SOUFFLÉ ROLL WITH VEGETABLE SAUCE

Here is a variation on the standard soufflé—one that is rolled like a jelly roll. It is not difficult to prepare and makes a terrific light meal with a salad or soup; it is of course a good source of calcium, iron, and vitamin A.

- ½ pound fresh spinach
- 1½ tablespoons margarine
- 1½ tablespoons flour
- 1½ cups skim milk
- 2 egg yolks
- ½ teaspoon dry mustard
- ½ teaspoon white pepper
- ¾ cup grated Fontina (about 4 ounces) or other low-fat cheese
- 1 tablespoon grated Parmesan
- 6 egg whites
- ¼ pound mushrooms, sliced
- 1 tablespoon safflower oil
- 1 cup Minted Vegetable Sauce (page 220)
  Fresh chopped parsley for garnish

Preheat the oven to 350°F. Oil an 8-by-12-inch Pyrex dish with a little vegetable oil. Cut a sheet of waxed paper to fit the bottom, lay it in the pan, and gently oil the top of the paper.

Wash the spinach well and cook in a pot of boiling water until just wilted, about 2 minutes. Drain well in a colander, pushing the excess water out with a spoon. When the spinach is cool enough to handle, take small clumps and squeeze out the remaining water with your hands. Dry on paper towels, and chop.

Melt the margarine in a saucepan and stir in the flour. Cook the mixture over low heat for 2 to 3 minutes, stirring constantly. Take the pan off the heat, pour in the milk, and whisk well to blend. Return the pan to the stove and cook the sauce, while stirring, until it thickens. Beat in the egg yolks, mustard, and pepper. Then stir in the cheeses, mixing until they melt. Fold in the spinach and keep warm.

Beat the egg whites until stiff. Gently fold in the cheese-spinach mixture with a spatula, and pour it into the prepared dish. Bake the soufflé for 25 minutes.

While the soufflé is cooking, sauté the mushrooms in the safflower oil. When the soufflé is done, invert it onto a dish towel and carefully peel off the waxed paper. Sprinkle the mushrooms over the soufflé. Roll the soufflé gently, like a jelly roll, pushing it over itself with the towel, and place the roll on a platter. Cover the soufflé roll with warm Minted Vegetable Sauce, and serve immediately, garnished with a little chopped parsley. *Serves 4.*

Calories: 348.9   Calcium: 500.9 mg.
Protein: 25.7 g.   Iron: 4.1 mg.
Fat: 19.5 g.   Sodium: 390.9 mg.
Carbohydrates: 20.5 g.   Potassium: 752.9 mg.
                         Vitamin A: 5,932.7 IU
                         Vitamin C: 45.9 mg.

CHEESE SOUFFLÉ

Everyone is intimidated by soufflés until they make one. They are in fact easily and quickly prepared and are among the best light meals. Here is a healthy variation of an old standard, which uses fewer egg yolks and Fontina cheese in place of Cheddar or Emmenthaler. Fontina has a distinctive flavor and less fat.

    1½ tablespoons margarine
    1½ tablespoons flour
    1½ cups skim milk
      2 egg yolks
     ½ teaspoon dry mustard
     ⅛ teaspoon cayenne
     ¾ cup grated Fontina (about 4 ounces), or other low-fat
        cheese
      1 tablespoon grated Parmesan
      6 egg whites

Preheat the oven to 350°F. Grease the bottom of a soufflé dish with a little safflower oil.

Melt the margarine in a saucepan. Add the flour, mix well, and cook over a low flame for 1 or 2 minutes, until the mixture begins to bubble. Take the pan off the heat, pour in the milk, and whisk until smooth. Return the pan to the heat and cook, stirring, until the mixture thickens. Stir in the egg yolks, mustard, and cayenne, then the cheeses. Mix until the cheeses melt, turn off the heat, and cover the pan.

Beat the egg whites until stiff. Gently fold in the cheese sauce with a spatula. Pour the mixture into the soufflé dish and bake for 30 minutes, or until the top is golden brown. Serve immediately. *Serves 4.*

Calories: 249.4   Calcium: 407.9 mg.
Protein: 19.9 g.   Iron: 1.1 mg.
Fat: 15.1 g.   Sodium: 318.6 mg.
Carbohydrates: 9.7 g. Potassium: 236.9 mg.
                       Vitamin A: 857.4 IU
                       Vitamin C: 0.8 mg.

ASPARAGUS SOUFFLÉ

Lemon juice and fresh dill go well with asparagus. This is a lighter soufflé than one made with egg yolks. Serve this protein-laden dish with lamb or veal.

½ pound asparagus
3 scallions, chopped
½ cup low-fat cottage cheese
2 tablespoons chopped fresh dill, or 1 teaspoon dried
3 tablespoons lemon juice
6 egg whites

Preheat the oven to 375°F. Lightly oil the bottom of a soufflé dish with safflower oil.

Fill a large frying pan three-quarters full with water and bring it to a boil. Place the asparagus carefully in the water after trimming off the white ends. Lower the heat and simmer until tender, about 3 to 5 minutes, depending on their size. Drain, and chop into large pieces.

Quickly purée the asparagus, scallions, cottage cheese, dill, and lemon juice together in a food processor or blender. You do not want the mixture to be completely smooth. Scrape into a bowl and reserve.

Beat the egg whites until stiff. Gently fold in the asparagus mixture. Pour the mixture into the soufflé dish and bake for 25 minutes. Serve immediately. *Serves 4.*

Calories: 92.1   Calcium: 60.4 mg.
Protein: 14.4 g.   Iron: 1 mg.
Fat: 0.5 g.   Sodium: 221.7 mg.
Carbohydrates: 6.7 g.   Potassium: 323.1 mg.
                        Vitamin A: 643.3 IU
                        Vitamin C: 27.3 mg.

BROCCOLI SOUFFLÉ

The standard soufflé is made with a white-sauce base. This variation substitutes cottage cheese, and thereby gives up many calories and much fat.

¾ pound broccoli
½ cup low-fat cottage cheese
1 clove garlic, minced
2 tablespoons grated Parmesan
  Pepper to taste
2 egg yolks
6 egg whites

Preheat the oven to 375°F. Lightly oil the bottom of a soufflé dish with a little safflower oil.

Cut off the lower stems of the broccoli. Steam the broccoli until tender. Purée the broccoli in a food processor or blender with the cottage and Parmesan cheeses, garlic, and pepper. Scrape the mixture into a bowl and stir in the egg whites.

Beat the egg whites until stiff. Gently fold in the broccoli mixture until it is just blended, then pour it into the soufflé dish. Bake for 20 to 25 minutes, or until the top is browned. Serve immediately. *Serves 4.*

Calories: 131.6
Protein: 15.8 g.
Fat: 5 g.
Carbohydrates: 6.1 g.

Calcium: 180.6 mg.
Iron: 1.5 mg.
Sodium: 220.8 mg.
Potassium: 377.8 mg.
Vitamin A: 2,021.6 IU
Vitamin C: 75.2 mg.

TOMATO, ONION, AND BASIL OMELETTE

Summer tomatoes and fresh basil make this omelette. The filling also works well as a sauce for poached sole. I use Fontina cheese because I like its flavor, but you can substitute any part-skim or low-sodium cheese.

    2 tablespoons safflower oil
    ½ onion, chopped
    1 tomato, peeled, seeded, and chopped (see page 85)
  1½ tablespoons chopped fresh basil, or ½ teaspoon dried
    2 egg yolks
    4 egg whites
    1 tablespoon seltzer
    1 ounce Fontina, grated, or other low-fat cheese
      Pepper to taste
      Fresh chopped parsley for garnish (optional)

Heat 1 tablespoon of the oil in a frying pan and sauté the onion until soft. Add the tomato and basil and cook another minute. Remove from the heat and keep warm.

Beat the egg yolks and egg whites with the seltzer. (The seltzer makes the omelette lighter.) Heat the remaining tablespoon of oil in an omelette pan until it is hot, then pour in the beaten eggs. Cook, stirring a few times and swirling the pan, so that it is evenly coated with eggs, until the eggs are almost cooked through.

Sprinkle a line of cheese down the center of the eggs, then top with the tomato-onion filling. Tilt the pan to a 45° angle from the burner and, using a fork, push one edge of the omelette so that it rolls over the filling and into a nice oval shape. Continue cooking over low heat for about 1 minute. Tilt the pan so that the omelette rolls onto a serving plate, and serve immediately, garnished with a little chopped parsley, if desired. *Serves 2.*

Calories: 305.1   Calcium: 180 mg.
Protein: 16.3 g.   Iron: 2.3 mg.
Fat: 22.8 g.   Sodium: 181.9 mg.
Carbohydrates: 10.5 g.   Potassium: 482.4 mg.
                         Vitamin A: 1,689.8 IU
                         Vitamin C: 33.4 mg.

ZUCCHINI–RED PEPPER OMELETTE

This has a simple, flavorful filling that also works well as a vegetable side dish for lamb.

      2 tablespoons safflower oil
      ½ red pepper, cut into thin strips
      1 small zucchini, halved and sliced
      1 clove garlic, minced
      ¼ teaspoon oregano
        Pepper to taste
      2 egg yolks
      4 egg whites
      1 tablespoon seltzer
      3 tablespoons grated Fontina
        Fresh chopped parsley for garnish

Heat 1 tablespoon oil in a small frying pan and sauté the red pepper until it is soft. Add the zucchini and cook until just tender. Stir in the garlic, oregano, and pepper. Remove from the heat and keep warm.

Beat the egg yolks, egg whites, and seltzer. Follow the instructions for cooking omelettes in the recipe for Tomato, Onion, and Basil Omelette on page 119. Serve immediately, garnished with a little chopped parsley. *Serves 2.*

        Calories: 299.1   Calcium: 155.6 mg.
        Protein: 16.4 g.   Iron: 2 mg.
        Fat: 22.8 g.   Sodium: 174 mg.
        Carbohydrates: 9.17 g.   Potassium: 367.2 mg.
                                 Vitamin A: 3,096 IU
                                 Vitamin C: 88.5 mg.

EGGPLANT OMELETTE

1 small eggplant (about ½ pound)
1 red pepper, seeded and chopped
1 large clove garlic
½ cup low-fat cottage cheese
½ teaspoon oregano
½ teaspoon pepper
2 tablespoons safflower oil
4 egg yolks
8 egg whites
3 tablespoons seltzer water
   Fresh chopped parsley for garnish

Prick the eggplant several times with a fork and bake in a preheated 350°F. oven until the center is soft. Remove the eggplant and let it sit until it is cool enough to handle. Cut the eggplant in half and scoop out the flesh.

Purée the eggplant with the red pepper, garlic, cottage cheese, oregano, and pepper until almost smooth. Scrape the mixture into a bowl.

Follow the instructions for making an omelette in the recipe for Tomato, Onion, and Basil Omelette on page 119, using 1 tablespoon oil, half the egg mixture, and half the filling. Slide the omelette carefully onto a plate and keep warm. Wipe out the pan with paper towels, heat the remaining tablespoon of oil, and make another omelette with the remaining eggs and filling. Serve the omelettes immediately, garnished with a little chopped parsley. *Serves 4.*

Calories: 214.8   Calcium: 66 mg.
Protein: 15.7 g.   Iron: 1.9 mg.
Fat: 13 g.   Sodium: 196.5 mg.
Carbohydrates: 9.9 g.   Potassium: 253.7 mg.
                         Vitamin A: 2,615.3 IU
                         Vitamin C: 70.5 mg.

EGGS FLORENTINE

1½ tablespoons margarine
1½ tablespoons flour
1½ cups skim milk
¼ teaspoon dry mustard
⅛ teaspoon cayenne
¾ cup grated Fontina (about 4 ounces)
1 tablespoon grated Parmesan
8 eggs
1 pound spinach

Preheat the oven to 350°F.

Melt the margarine in a saucepan and stir in the flour. Cook over low heat for a few minutes, until the mixture just begins to bubble. Take the pan off the heat, pour in the milk, and whisk until smooth. Return the pan to the heat and cook, stirring constantly, until the sauce has thickened, about 2 to 3 minutes. Add the mustard, cayenne, and cheeses, and stir until the cheeses have melted. Cover the pan and remove from the heat.

Poach the eggs in an egg poacher or use a frying pan. If using a frying pan, fill it with water about three-quarters full. Add 2 tablespoons vinegar and heat the water until it simmers. Break each egg into a little dish and slide it gently into the water, 4 at a time. As the eggs are poaching, fold the whites gently over the yolks with a spoon and simmer for 3 minutes. Do not let the water come to a boil. Drain the eggs on paper towels.

Wash the spinach well. In a large pot, boil 1 cup of water, add the spinach, and cook, stirring, until it has just wilted. Drain in a colander, rinse with cold water, then press out the water with the back of a spoon. Using your hand, take small clumps of spinach and squeeze out any excess water. Drain on paper towels.

Lightly oil a baking dish with safflower oil. Chop the spinach and spread evenly over the bottom. Lay the poached eggs on top of the spinach and cover each egg with a little cheese sauce. Bake for 10 to 15 minutes. *Serves 4.*

Calories: 380

Protein: 28.9 g.

Fat: 24 g.

Carbohydrates: 15 g.

Calcium: 550.3 mg.

Iron: 6.2 mg.

Sodium: 432.3 mg.

Potassium: 808.8 mg.

Vitamin A: 10,927.4 units

Vitamin C: 58.5 mg.

Fourteen

Fish

LEMON DILL–BROILED FILLETS

    3 tablespoons lemon juice
    2 tablespoons white wine
    1 shallot, minced
    1 tablespoon chopped fresh dill, or ½ teaspoon dried
    4 fillets, such as flounder or sole (about 1 pound)
       Fresh chopped parsley or watercress sprigs for garnish

Preheat the broiler.

Combine the lemon juice, wine, shallots, and dill. Lay the fillets in a large baking pan and sprinkle with the lemon-dill mixture. Broil for 2 to 3 minutes, or until the fish flakes at the touch of a fork. Serve garnished with watercress sprigs or chopped parsley. *Serves 4.*

Calories: 103.6	Calcium: 19.8 mg.
Protein: 19.2 g.	Iron: 1.1 mg.
Fat: 0.9 g.	Sodium: 91 mg.
Carbohydrates: 5.1 g.	Potassium: 438.5 mg.
	Vitamin A: 96.7 IU
	Vitamin C: 6 mg.

FILLETS WITH VEGETABLES

　1½　tablespoons safflower oil
　½　onion, thinly sliced
　¼　red pepper, seeded and cut into thin strips
　2　cloves garlic, minced
　2　tomatoes, peeled, seeded, and chopped (see page 85)
　¼　small eggplant, julienned
　1　zucchini, julienned
　1　tablespoon grated fresh ginger
　½　cup white wine
　1　tablespoon finely chopped fresh basil, or ½ teaspoon
　　　dried
　1　tablespoon fresh lemon juice
　4　skinned and boned fillets, such as sole, flounder, striped
　　　bass, or red snapper, about 1 pound
　　　Chopped fresh parsley for garnish

Preheat the oven to 350°F.

Heat the oil in a large saucepan and sauté the onion and pepper. Add the garlic, tomatoes, and eggplant, and cook, stirring constantly, until the eggplant is soft. Add the zucchini and cook, stirring constantly, until soft. Add the ginger, wine, basil, and lemon juice, and simmer for 5 minutes.

Rinse the fillets under cold water and pat dry on paper towels. Lightly oil a roasting pan and lay the fillets on the bottom. Divide the vegetables evenly over each fillet, and bake for 12 to 15 minutes, or until the fish flakes at the touch of a fork. Transfer the fillets carefully to plates, and serve garnished with parsley. *Serves 4.*

Calories: 211.1　　　　Calcium: 59.5 mg.
Protein: 21.8 g.　　　 Iron: 2.2 mg.
Fat: 6.7 g.　　　　　　Sodium: 97.7 mg.
Carbohydrates: 15.1 g.　Potassium: 894.2 mg.
　　　　　　　　　　　Vitamin A: 1,433.7 IU
　　　　　　　　　　　Vitamin C: 57.1 mg.

POACHED SOLE WITH BEET SAUCE

This unusual and very colorful nouvelle cuisine sauce is the calorie-counter's dream.

    SAUCE:
    2 beets
    2 cups Chicken Broth (page 87), or canned low-sodium
      broth
    3 cups orange juice

    4 sole fillets, about 1 pound
    4 scallions
    2 tablespoons grated fresh ginger
    4 tablespoons white wine
    2 tablepoons lemon juice
      Watercress for garnish (optional)

Remove the beet greens and roots and scrub the beets well. Cook the beets in a large saucepan of water until they are tender, about 30 to 45 minutes. Remove the beets, let them cool, then peel off the skin and reserve the beets.

Bring the broth and orange juice to a boil in a saucepan and reduce the liquid by half.

Purée the beets in a food processor. Add the liquid and process just to mix. Pour the sauce back into the pan and keep warm.

Preheat the oven to 350 °F.

Rinse the fillets under cold water and pat dry on paper towels. Lay each on a square of aluminum foil.

Remove the green tops of the scallions and cut the white parts into julienne strips. Divide the scallions over each fillet, and top with grated ginger.

Sprinkle each fillet with wine and lemon juice. Fold up the foil into packages, and bake for 20 minutes.

Spoon the sauce into 4 plates, spreading it evenly over the bottom. Carefully transfer the fillets onto the sauce, and decorate with a few sprigs of watercress, if desired. *Serves 4.*

Calories: 222.7   Calcium: 54.6 mg.
Protein: 22.7 g.   Iron: 2.2 mg.
Fat: 1.4 g.   Sodium: 178.7 mg.
Carbohydrates: 30 g.   Potassium: 902 mg.
                           Vitamin A: 341.1 IU
                           Vitamin C: 91.7 mg.

FILLETS WITH BASIL AND ROSEMARY

    1½ tablespoons safflower oil
     3 shallots, chopped
     4 thin fillets, such as sole or flounder (about 1 pound)
     3 tablespoons chopped fresh basil, or 1½ teaspoons dried
     ½ teaspoon rosemary
        Pepper to taste
     4 tablespoons white wine
     3 tablespoons lemon juice
        Fresh chopped parsley or sorrel for garnish

Preheat the oven to 350°F.

Oil the bottom of a casserole and sprinkle the shallots over the bottom.

Rinse the fillets under cold water and pat dry on paper towels. Sprinkle each with the basil, rosemary, and a little pepper. Then, taking the wider end, gently roll each fillet and put it in the casserole.

Pour the wine and the lemon juice over the fillets and bake, basting a few times, for 20 minutes, or until the fish flakes easily. Serve garnished with a little fresh parsley or chopped sorrel, if available. *Serves 4.*

Calories: 166.8   Calcium: 30.6 mg.
Protein: 19.7 g.   Iron: 1.5 mg.
Fat: 6 g.   Sodium: 94.2 mg.
Carbohydrates: 10.9 g.   Potassium: 512 mg.
                             Vitamin A: 289.9 IU
                             Vitamin C: 11.1 mg.

SOLE STUFFED WITH
BROCCOLI WITH HERBED TOMATO SAUCE

This recipe also works well with spinach, but broccoli is both more unusual and more nutritious.

¼ pound broccoli flowerets
1 shallot, minced
4 fillets of sole or flounder, boned and skinned, about 1
   pound
1 cup Herbed Tomato Sauce (page 185)
2 tablespoons chopped chives for garnish (optional)

Preheat the oven to 350°F. Lightly oil a baking dish, using safflower oil.

Separate the broccoli into small flowerets and steam until just tender, about 2 to 3 minutes. Sprinkle the chopped shallot in a line across the large end of each fillet and top with a few broccoli flowerets. Roll up the fillets and lay them in the baking dish.

Pour the tomato sauce over each fillet, cover, and bake for 15 to 20 minutes, depending on the thickness of the fish. Serve sprinkled with a little chopped chives, if desired. *Serves 4.*

Calories: 125.5   Calcium: 48.3 mg.
Protein: 20.5 g.   Iron: 1.6 mg.
Fat: 2.2 g.   Sodium: 95.6 mg.
Carbohydrates: 5.5 g.   Potassium: 638.8 mg.
                         Vitamin A: 989.3 IU
                         Vitamin C: 38.7 mg.

POACHED SOLE WITH TOMATOES AND MUSHROOMS

    1 tablespoon safflower oil
    4 scallions, chopped
    ¼ pound mushrooms, washed and chopped (caps and
       stems)
    2 cloves garlic, minced
    ½ cup white wine
    3 tablespoons fresh lemon juice
    2 tomatoes, peeled, seeded, and chopped (see page 85)
    3 tablespoons chopped fresh parsley
    4 fillets sole or flounder, boned and skinned, about 1 pound
      Chopped parsley for garnish (optional)

Preheat oven to 350°F.

In a frying pan, heat the oil and, over low heat, sauté the scallions and mushrooms until tender, about 2 to 3 minutes. Add the garlic, wine, and lemon juice and bring the liquid to a boil. Let the liquid reduce until it has almost evaporated. Lower the heat, stir in the tomatoes and parsley, and cook another 2 minutes.

Lay each fillet on a sheet of aluminum foil and cover with the tomato-mushroom mixture. Fold up the foil tightly and bake for 20 minutes. Transfer the fillets carefully to plates, and garnish with a little chopped parsley, if desired. *Serves 4.*

Calories: 184.3   Calcium: 44.6 mg.
Protein: 21.4 g.   Iron: 2.1 mg.
Fat: 4.6 g.   Sodium: 100.4 mg.
Carbohydrates: 11.8 g. Potassium: 853 mg.
                  Vitamin A: 937.4 IU
                  Vitamin C: 36.6 mg.

BLACKENED REDFISH

This spicy Cajun recipe calls for dipping the fish first in herbs, then in clarified butter. We use safflower oil, which works just as well without the fat and cholesterol. This is an excellent but fiery combination of pepper and herbs that needs a thick fish to soften the bite.

    4 redfish fillets, or other thick fillets, such as scrod or cod,
      boned and skinned (about 1 pound)
    1 teaspoon black pepper
    ½ teaspoon white pepper
    1 teaspoon thyme
    ⅛ teaspoon cayenne
    2 teaspoons chili powder
    3 tablespoons safflower oil
      Lemon slices for garnish
      Fresh chopped parsley for garnish

Rinse the fillets under cold water and dry on paper towels. Mix the spices in a bowl and spread out evenly on a plate. On another plate, spread the oil. Dip each fillet first in the spices, turning to coat evenly on both sides, then in the oil.

Heat a large cast-iron frying pan until white ash forms. Carefully lay the fillets in the pan and cook about 2 to 3 minutes a side, depending on the thickness. Serve garnished with lemon slices and a little chopped parsley. *Serves 4.*

    Calories: 120.8   Calcium: 3.5 mg.
    Protein: 6.2 g.   Iron: 0.2 mg.
    Fat: 10.4 g.   Sodium: 25 mg.
    Carbohydrates: 0   Potassium: 134.4 mg.
                         Vitamin A: 0 I
                         Vitamin C: 0.8 mg.

RED SNAPPER
WITH MINTED ORANGE SAUCE

Red snapper goes particularly well with fruit sauce; however, any fillet can be substituted.

SAUCE:
- 1 tablespoon safflower oil
- 4 scallions, sliced
- 1 clove garlic, minced
- 1 tablespoon grated fresh ginger, or ½ teaspoon ground ginger
- 1 cup Chicken Broth (page 87), or canned low-sodium broth
- 1 cup orange juice
- 1 tablespoon fresh lemon juice
- 1 tablespoon grated orange rind
- 1 teaspoon grated lemon rind

- 4 red snapper fillets, about 1 pound
- ½ cup white wine
- 1 cup water
- 1 tablespoon lemon juice
- 2–3 sprigs parsley
- 2 tablespoons finely chopped fresh mint, or 1 teaspoon dried

Heat the oil in a small saucepan and sauté the scallion. Add the remaining sauce ingredients and simmer for 30 minutes. Keep warm.

Rinse the fillets under cold water and dry them on paper towels. In a fish poacher or roasting pan, bring the wine, water, lemon juice, and parsley to a boil, then reduce heat until the liquid simmers. Lay the fillets gently in the pan and poach for 5 to 6 minutes, or until the fish flakes at the touch of a fork.

Remove the fish from the pan and cover with sauce. *Serves 4.*

Calories: 188.1
Protein: 24.2 g.
Fat: 4.6 g.
Carbohydrates: 15.8 g.

Calcium: 40.2 mg.
Iron: 1.7 mg.
Sodium: 11.7 mg.
Potassium: 557.6 mg.
Vitamin A: 303.7 IU
Vitamin C: 36.5 mg.

TROUT WITH ORANGE SAUCE

My brother eats trout with maple syrup, a taste developed after too many fishing breakfasts of pancakes and trout. This recipe came about in an effort to change his taste. It didn't. Nonetheless, trout is an excellent fish—it is light, sweetly mild, and high in protein with no carbohydrates.

> 4 small trout (about ¾ pound each), cleaned
> 3 tablespoons safflower oil
> 4 shallots, finely chopped
> ½ cup white wine
> 3 cups orange juice
> 3 tablespoons lemon juice
> ½ cup Brown Stock (page 222), or canned low-sodium beef broth
> 1 orange, peeled and sectioned
> Chopped parsley

Rinse the trout inside and out under cold water and dry on paper towels.

Heat 2 tablespoons safflower oil in a large frying pan (preferably nonstick) and cook the trout (2 at a time if the pan cannot hold all 4) until they are golden brown on the bottom, about 5 minutes. Carefully flip the trout and cook until brown on the other side. Remove the trout and keep warm while you make the sauce.

Heat the remaining tablespoon oil in a saucepan and sauté the shallots until they are soft. Add the wine and the orange and lemon juices, bring the liquid to a boil, and let it reduce by a quarter. Lower the heat, stir in the brown stock, and simmer another 1 or 2 minutes.

Ladle the sauce onto 4 plates and lay the trout carefully on top. Garnish with orange sections and chopped parsley. *Serves 4.*

Calories: 415.5	Calcium: 50.6 mg.
Protein: 35.6 g.	Iron: 1.4 mg.
Fat: 14.5 g.	Sodium: 37.7 mg.
Carbohydrates: 29.9 g.	Potassium: 601.6 mg.
	Vitamin A: 2,172.3 IU
	Vitamin C: 94.6 mg.

COLD POACHED SALMON
WITH PESTO SAUCE

COURT BOUILLON:
   7–8 cups water
   ½ cup white wine
   10 peppercorns
   1 lemon, sliced
   4–5 sprigs parsley
   1 bay leaf

   4 small salmon fillets (about 1½ pounds)
   1 cup Tofu Mayonnaise (page 227)
   ¼ cup Pesto (page 221)
   Lemon slices
   Fresh chopped parsley

In a large poaching or roasting pan, combine the court bouillon ingredients, adding more water, if necessary, so that the salmon fillets will be covered. Bring the liquid to a boil, then lower the heat until it barely simmers. Carefully lay the salmon in the pan and poach for 5 minutes, or until the salmon is cooked through. Lift the salmon out gently with a spatula and place on a plate, cover, and refrigerate until cool.

Combine the Tofu Mayonnaise and the Pesto in a small bowl. Serve the salmon with the sauce, garnished with lemon slices and chopped parsley. *Serves 4.*

Calories: 376.5
Protein: 30.1 g.
Fat: 27.3 g.
Carbohydrates: 14.7 g.
Calcium: 166.9 mg.
Iron: 2.3 mg.
Sodium: 5.7 mg.
Potassium: 78.2 mg.
Vitamin A: 283.4 IU
Vitamin C: 16.3 mg.

BOUILLABAISSE

A simple, exquisite adaptation of the hearty classic, divinely low in calories. This dish improves in flavor if it sits a day or two, and can easily be frozen.

      1 pound cod
      ½ pound mussels
      ½ pound shrimp
      ½ pound bay scallops
      1 tablespoon safflower oil
      2 large shallots, finely chopped
      3 large cloves garlic, minced
    4-5 tomatoes, peeled, seeded, and chopped (see page 85)
      4 cups fish stock (available in most fish stores)
      ½ cup white wine
      1 tablespoon fresh basil, finely chopped, or ½ teaspoon dried
      ¼ teaspoon thyme
      ¼ teaspoon red pepper flakes
        Pinch saffron
      1 teaspoon pepper
      1 bay leaf
        Chopped parsley for garnish

Scrub the mussels well, discarding any that have opened. Peel and devein the shrimp. Cut the cod into small pieces.

Heat the oil in a large saucepan and sauté the shallots until wilted. Add the garlic and tomatoes and cook, stirring constantly, for 1 minute. Add the stock, wine, and remaining spices. Bring the liquid to a boil, reduce the heat, and simmer for 15 minutes.

Add the cod and simmer 5 minutes. Then add the shrimp and scallops and simmer another 5 minutes. Add the mussels, cover, and simmer just until the mussels have opened, about 5 to 7 minutes more. Serve garnished with chopped parsley. *Serves 6.*

Calories: 168.2   Calcium: 63.4 mg.
Protein: 18.8 g.   Iron: 2.6 mg.
Fat: 0.1 g.   Sodium: 189.8 mg.
Carbohydrates: 11.6 g.   Potassium: 704.8 mg.
                         Vitamin A: 957.7 IU
                         Vitamin C: 32.5 mg.

STEAMED MUSSELS

Several years ago I spent an afternoon scraping tiny mussels off the rocks on a beach in Brittany with a friend. That night we concocted this recipe over a campfire.

    2 pounds mussels
    1 tablespoon olive oil
    3 large shallots, minced
    1 leek, white part, chopped
    3 garlic cloves, minced
    1 cup white wine
    ½ cup water
    ½ teaspoon thyme
    1 bay leaf
    4 tablespoons minced parsley
       Chopped parsley for garnish (optional)

Scrub the mussels well, discarding any that are open.

Heat the oil in a large pot and sauté the shallots and leek until they are wilted. Add the garlic, wine, water, thyme, bay leaf, and parsley, and simmer for 5 minutes.

Add the mussels, cover the pot, and simmer until the mussels have opened, about 5 to 7 minutes. Divide the mussels on 4 large plates, strain the liquid, and ladle it over the mussels. Garnish with chopped parsley, if desired. *Serves 4.*

    Calories: 174.5   Calcium: 96.7 mg.
    Protein: 11.1 g.   Iron: 3.4 mg.
    Fat: 4.9 g.   Sodium: 199.6 mg.
    Carbohydrates: 13 g.   Potassium: 488.2 mg.
                           Vitamin A: 387.5 IU
                           Vitamin C: 15.3 mg.

SCALLOPS IN GARLIC SAUCE

Here is a Hunan garlic sauce without excessive oil and soy sauce. It is light, and the hot chili oil gives it a subtle bite. Serve it as well with shrimp or chicken.

    1 pound bay scallops
    1 pound broccoli
 2½ tablespoons peanut oil
    3 garlic cloves, minced
    2 tablespoons grated fresh ginger
   ¼ teaspoon hot chili oil (optional)

Rinse the scallops and pat dry on paper towels. Separate the broccoli into flowerets, discarding or reserving the stems for soup. Steam the broccoli flowerets until just tender, remove from the heat, and keep warm.

In a large frying pan or wok heat the peanut oil and quickly sauté the garlic and ginger. Add the scallops and sauté, stirring constantly until they are tender and cooked through, about 2 minutes. Add the broccoli and the hot chili oil, if desired, lower the heat, and cook until the broccoli is heated. Serve with brown rice, if desired. *Serves 4.*

Calories: 201.5   Calcium: 124.2 mg.
Protein: 20.9 g.   Iron: 3.3 mg.
Fat: 9 g.   Sodium: 304 mg.
Carbohydrates: 11.4 g.   Potassium: 838.2 mg.
                         Vitamin A: 2,211 IU
                         Vitamin C: 101.1 mg.

COLD SEAFOOD WITH SAFFRON SAUCE

This recipe was inspired by Moroccan cuisine, in particular by an overwhelming supply of saffron that was brought to me by a friend who visited that country. Saffron can be expensive here; curry powder can be used in its place.

½ pound shrimp
¾ cup water
¼ cup white wine
3 tablespoons lemon juice
1 shallot, minced
½ pound bay scallops
 Lettuce leaves
 Fresh fruit slices

SAFFRON SAUCE:
1 cup low-fat yogurt
½ cup fresh orange juice
4 tablespoons fresh lemon juice
 Pinch saffron
½ teaspoon turmeric
⅛ teaspoon ginger

Clean and devein the shrimp. In a saucepan, bring the water, wine, lemon juice, and shallot to a boil, then lower the heat until the liquid barely simmers and add the scallops and shrimp. Poach the seafood for 3 to 4 minutes, until the shrimp is pink and tender. Drain and chill until ready to use.

To prepare the sauce, mix the yogurt, orange and lemon juices, saffron, tumeric, and ginger together, and pour it over the seafood. (The sauce can be made ahead of time and kept in the refrigerator until ready to use.) Toss well and serve on a bed of lettuce, garnished with fruit slices. *Serves 4.*

Calories: 130.3
Protein: 18.1 g.
Fat: 1.5 g.
Carbohydrates: 10.4 g.

Calcium: 109.4 mg.
Iron: 1.8 mg.
Sodium: 230.2 mg.
Potassium: 488.2 mg.
Vitamin A: 94.5 IU
Vitamin C: 20.6 mg.

Fifteen

Poultry

POACHED CHICKEN BREASTS

Use these chicken breasts for salad or for any cold chicken dish. Save the broth for other recipes.

    4 chicken breasts (about 2 pounds)
    1 onion, quartered
    2 carrots, quartered
    1 leek, white part only, chopped
  5-6 cups water
  4-6 peppercorns

Put the chicken, vegetables, water (and more if it doesn't cover), and the peppercorns in a large saucepan. Bring the water to a boil, then immediately lower the heat and simmer, without boiling, for 15 to 20 minutes, until the breasts are cooked through.

Drain the chicken, chill the liquid, skim off the fat that congeals on the surface, and reserve for broth. When cool enough to handle, remove the skin of the chicken.

Calories: 166   Calcium: 11 mg.
Protein: 31.6 g.   Iron: 1.6 mg.
Fat: 3.4 g.   Sodium: 64 mg.
Carbohydrates: 0   Potassium: 411 mg.
                       Vitamin A: 60 IU
                       Vitamin C: 0

LEMON CHICKEN
WITH BASIL AND OREGANO

The combination of lemon with fresh basil and garlic works particularly well not only for chicken, but also for fish. Here I've added oregano; use fresh if you can find it.

> 4 Poached Chicken Breasts (preceding recipe), skin removed
> ½ tablespoon safflower oil
> 1 clove garlic, minced
> ¾ cup Chicken Broth (page 87), or canned low-sodium broth
> ¼ cup white wine
> 2½ tablespoons lemon juice
> 2 tablespoons chopped fresh basil, or 1 teaspoon dried
> 1 teaspoon chopped fresh oregano, or ⅛ teaspoon dried
> ½ teaspoon pepper

Keep the skinned chicken breasts warm.

In a frying pan, heat the oil and sauté the garlic for 30 seconds. Add the broth and the wine, bring the liquid to a boil, and let it reduce by half. Lower the heat and stir in the lemon juice, basil, oregano, and pepper. Add the chicken breasts, rib side up, and heat through. Serve with a little sauce spooned over each breast. *Serves 4.*

Calories: 204.6   Calcium: 19.9 mg.
Protein: 32.5 g.   Iron: 1.7 mg.
Fat: 5.1 g.   Sodium: 90.7 mg.
Carbohydrates: 1.7 g.   Potassium: 455.3 mg.
                         Vitamin A: 253.3 IU
                         Vitamin C: 7 mg.

CHICKEN PROVENÇALE

    4 chicken breasts (about 2 pounds), skin removed
    1 tablespoon olive oil
    1 onion, chopped
    1 green pepper, seeds removed, cut in strips
 6-8 mushrooms, chopped
    ½ cup white wine
    ½ cup Chicken Broth (page 87), or canned low-sodium broth
    4 tomatoes, peeled, seeded, and chopped (see page 85)
    1 tablespoon tomato paste
    3 cloves garlic, minced
    2 tablespoons chopped fresh basil, or 1 teaspoon dried
    ¼ teaspoon marjoram
    ½ teaspoon thyme
    1 bay leaf
     Chopped parsley for garnish (optional)

Preheat the oven to 350°F.

In a large, nonstick frying pan heat the oil and brown the chicken. Remove the breasts and place them in a large casserole.

Add the onion and green pepper to the frying pan and sauté until soft. Add the mushrooms, cooking until soft. Pour in the wine and chicken broth, bring the liquid to a boil, and let it reduce until it has almost evaporated.

Stir in the tomatoes, tomato paste, garlic, and herbs, and cook another few minutes. Pour the sauce over the chicken, cover, and bake for 30 minutes. Remove the breasts, cover each with sauce, and serve garnished with parsley, if desired. *Serves 4.*

Calories: 317.8   Calcium: 63.9 mg.
Protein: 36.9 g.   Iron: 3.7 mg.
Fat: 7.3 g.   Sodium: 106.7 mg.
Carbohydrates: 21.2 g.   Potassium: 1,282.4 mg.
                    Vitamin A: 1,856.2 IU
                    Vitamin C: 115.6 mg.

CHICKEN WITH EGGPLANT

Because of its assertive flavor, eggplant is often found in combination with lamb or as a side dish to a meat entrée. However, it can also complement the delicate taste of chicken without overpowering it.

Eggplant contains a good deal of water, which can be drawn out by salting the eggplant before cooking and letting the slices sit in a colander for half an hour. This also prevents the eggplant from absorbing too much oil.

    1 small eggplant
    1 tablespoon olive oil
    1 tablespoon safflower oil
    4 chicken breasts (about 2 pounds), skin removed
    2 shallots, finely chopped
    3 tomatoes, peeled, seeded, and chopped (see page 85)
    4 cloves garlic, minced
    1 tablespoon fine herbs
 1½ tablespoons chopped fresh basil, chopped, or 1½
       teaspoons dried
    ¼ cup white wine
    ¾ cup Chicken Broth (page 87), or canned low-sodium
       broth
       Chopped parsley for garnish (optional)

Preheat the oven to 350°F.

Slice the eggplant, sprinkle with salt, and let drain in a colander for a half hour. Rinse them well, then pat dry on paper towels to remove salt, and cut the eggplant into cubes.

In a frying pan, heat the oils and sauté the chicken breasts for a minute to brown. Remove the breasts and place in a large casserole. Sauté the shallots until soft. Add the eggplant and cook, stirring frequently, until soft. Add the tomatoes, garlic, and herbs, and cook another 2 minutes. Stir in the wine and broth.

Pour the eggplant mixture over the chicken, cover the casserole, and bake for 35 minutes. Remove the breasts, cover each with the eggplant mixture, and serve garnished with parsley, if desired. *Serves 4.*

Calories: 317.2   Calcium: 53 mg.
Protein: 35.5 g.   Iron: 3.2 mg.
Fat: 10.6 g.   Sodium: 98.1 mg.
Carbohydrates: 16 g.   Potassium: 1,030.6 mg.
                       Vitamin A: 1,181.7 IU
                       Vitamin C: 42.6 mg.

CHICKEN WITH HERBS AND MUSHROOMS

The brown stock, herbs, and mushrooms give this chicken a gamy taste that makes it a good winter entrée. Low-sodium canned beef broth can always be substituted but the flavor is not commensurate. You can also use this sauce with quail or Cornish game hens.

    1 tablespoon safflower oil
    4 chicken breasts (about 2 pounds), skin removed
    2 shallots, minced
    1 pound mushrooms, washed and sliced
    ½ cup white wine
    1 cup Brown Stock (page 222), or canned low-sodium beef
       broth
    1 teaspoon rosemary
    ½ teaspoon marjoram
      Chopped parsley for garnish (optional)

Preheat the oven to 350°F.

Heat the oil in a large saucepan, brown the chicken, then remove and place in a large casserole.

Sauté the shallots in the oil, then add the mushrooms and cook until they are soft, stirring frequently. Pour in the wine and bring it to a boil, letting it reduce by half. Stir in the brown stock and herbs, and simmer for 5 minutes.

Pour the sauce over the chicken and bake for 35 minutes. Remove the breasts, top with the mushroom sauce, and serve garnished with parsley, if desired. *Serves 4.*

Calories: 338.6   Calcium: 62.1 mg.
Protein: 38.2 g.   Iron: 3.6 mg.
Fat: 8.3 g.   Sodium: 144.6 mg.
Carbohydrates: 17.3 g.   Potassium: 1,205.3 mg.
                            Vitamin A: 3,744.3 IU
                            Vitamin C: 17.3 mg.

CHICKEN STROGANOFF

I first tried yogurt in a stroganoff one night several years ago when I ran out of sour cream; later I tried the recipe with chicken instead of beef. The result is a fine and piquant variation of the classic recipe.

    1½ tablespoons safflower oil
     4 chicken breasts (about 2 pounds), skin removed
     1 onion, cut in half, then into eighths
    ¾ pound mushrooms, sliced
     1 cup Chicken Broth (page 87), or canned low-sodium broth
    ½ cup white wine
    ¾ cup low-fat yogurt
     1 tablespoon chopped fresh dill
        Pepper to taste

Remove the chicken from the bones and cut into strips. Heat the oil in a large frying pan and quickly sauté the chicken on both sides until it just turns white. Remove and drain on paper towels.

Add the onion and mushrooms to the pan (add a little more oil if needed) and sauté until tender. Pour in the broth and the wine, bring the liquid to a boil, and let it reduce until about ½ cup remains.

Add the chicken to the onion-mushroom mixture and stir in the yogurt, dill, and pepper. Let the stroganoff simmer for 15 to 20 minutes, until the chicken is cooked through. Serve over spinach noodles or wild or brown rice. *Serves 4.*

Calories: 307.5   Calcium: 87.8 mg.
Protein: 36.9 g.   Iron: 2.7 mg.
Fat: 9.5 g.   Sodium: 136.8 mg.
Carbohydrates: 11.4 g.   Potassium: 914.8 mg.
                         Vitamin A: 206 IU
                         Vitamin C: 10.2 mg.

STUFFED CHICKEN BREASTS WITH MINTED VEGETABLE SAUCE

The fresh mint and peas in this sauce liven up the taste of chicken. This simple and light recipe makes an elegant entrée rich in iron, potassium, and vitamin A.

    4 chicken breasts (about 2 pounds), skin removed
    1 carrot, finely julienned
    1 leek, white part only, finely julienned
    2 scallions, finely julienned
    4 tablespoons white wine
    2 cups Minted Vegetable Sauce (page 220)
    ¼ pound snow peas

Preheat the oven to 350°F.

Tear off 4 large squares of aluminum foil and lay a chicken breast in the center of each. Top each breast with a little carrot, leek, and scallion, then sprinkle some wine over each. Fold up the foil well, and bake for 25 minutes.

While the chicken is cooking, make the sauce and steam the snow peas until just tender, about 3 minutes.

Divide the sauce between 4 plates and spread across the bottom. Make a pinwheel in the center with the snow peas. Carefully remove the breasts from the foil and lay them on top of the snow peas. *Serves 4.*

    Calories: 317.8   Calcium: 138.5 mg.
    Protein: 40.2 g.   Iron: 4.3 mg.
    Fat: 5.6 g.   Sodium: 134.8 mg.
    Carbohydrates: 30.6 g.   Potassium: 943.9 mg.
                             Vitamin A: 5,155.2 IU
                             Vitamin C: 45.5 mg.

CHICKEN FLORENTINE

    4 chicken breasts (about 2 pounds), skin removed
    2 ounces Fontina, or other low-fat cheese, grated
1½ cups Chicken Broth (page 87), or canned low-sodium
        broth
    ½ cup white wine

SAUCE:
    1 pound spinach
    2 shallots, chopped
1½ cups Chicken Broth, or canned low-sodium broth
        Pepper to taste

    ¼ pound mushrooms, sliced (optional)

Preheat the oven to 350°F.

With a sharp knife, make a deep slit lengthwise in each of the chicken breasts and fill the pocket with cheese. In a flat casserole, bring 1½ cups broth and the wine to a boil, and lower the heat until the liquid simmers. Add the chicken, pocket side up, cover, and poach in the oven for 20 minutes, or until the chicken is cooked through. Remove the chicken from the liquid and keep warm, reserving the liquid for the sauce.

While the chicken is cooking make the sauce: Wash the spinach well in a colander under cold water. In a large saucepan, bring 1½ cups broth and poaching liquid to a boil. Add the spinach and shallots, and cook, stirring occasionally, for 15 minutes. Purée the spinach sauce in a blender or food processor, return to the pan, and season to taste with pepper.

Ladle the sauce onto 4 plates, lay a chicken breast on top of each plate, and garnish with sliced mushrooms, if desired. *Serves 4.*

Calories: 301   Calcium: 249.3 mg.
Protein: 41.7 g.   Iron: 6.1 mg.
Fat: 6.8 g.   Sodium: 297.3 mg.
Carbohydrates: 8.7 g.   Potassium: 1,020.1 mg.
                         Vitamin A: 6,887.5 IU
                         Vitamin C: 58.9 mg.

ORANGE CHICKEN

3 shallots, finely chopped
1 cup fresh orange juice
3 tablespoons lemon juice
2 tablespoons grated fresh ginger
2 tablespoons Dijon mustard
2 garlic cloves, minced
4 chicken breasts (about 2 pounds), skin removed
   Orange slices for garnish
   Watercress sprigs for garnish

SAUCE:
½ cup fresh orange juice
2 tablespoons lemon juice
½ cup Brown Stock (page 222), or canned low-sodium beef broth

Combine the shallots, 1 cup orange juice, 3 tablespoons lemon juice, ginger, mustard, and garlic and pour over the chicken breasts. Cover and let marinate at room temperature for 6 hours or overnight in the refrigerator.

Preheat the oven to 350°F. Drain the chicken, reserving the marinade for the sauce, and bake for 35 to 40 minutes, until the chicken is done. (You can also cook the chicken over a grill, about 10 to 12 minutes a side.)

While the chicken is cooking, make the sauce: Mix the marinade with ½ cup orange juice, 2 tablespoons lemon juice, and brown stock in a saucepan. Bring the liquid to a boil and let it reduce by a third. Pour a little sauce over the chicken, and serve garnished with orange slices and watercress. *Serves 4.*

Calories: 279.3
Protein: 35.6 g.
Fat: 5.2 g.
Carbohydrates: 20.5 g.
Calcium: 69.5 mg.
Iron: 2.8 mg.
Sodium: 296.5 mg.
Potassium: 868.6 mg.
Vitamin A: 2,068.4 IU
Vitamin C: 55.9 mg.

SESAME CHICKEN

   3 Poached Chicken Breasts (page 141), skin removed
1½ pound asparagus, cut into 1-inch pieces
   4 scallions, julienned
1½ tablespoons sesame oil
   2 cloves garlic, minced
1½ tablespoons grated fresh ginger
   2 tablespoons lemon juice
1½ tablespoons toasted sesame seeds

Remove the bones from the poached breasts and cut the meat into 2-inch long strips. Steam the asparagus and scallions until just tender, about 3 to 4 minutes. Remove from the heat and keep warm.

In a large saucepan or wok, heat the oil and add the garlic and ginger. Cook for 30 seconds, then add the asparagus, chicken, and lemon juice. Cook, stirring constantly, just to heat through. Stir in the sesame seeds. Serve with brown rice, if desired. *Serves 4.*

Calories: 227.4   Calcium: 27.2 mg.
Protein: 27.2 g.   Iron: 11.4 mg.
Fat: 9.7 g.   Sodium: 54.3 mg.
Carbohydrates: 9.1 g. Potassium: 642.3 mg.
                     Vitamin A: 900.7 IU
                     Vitamin C: 42.3 mg.

CHICKEN CURRY

This simple recipe is one my mother served at dinner parties. I use my own chutney, but any will do.

> 1½ cups orange juice
> 1 teaspoon cinnamon
> 2–3 teaspoons curry powder
> ¼ cup raisins
> ¼ cup Apple-Peach Chutney (page 230)
> 4 chicken breasts (about 2 pounds), skin removed
> 1½ ounces slivered almonds

Preheat the oven to 350°F.

Mix the orange juice, cinnamon, curry powder, raisins, and chutney in a bowl. Place the chicken breasts in a casserole and pour the sauce over each.

Cover the casserole and bake for 35 to 40 minutes, until the chicken is done. Serve the chicken with a little sauce spooned over the top, garnished with slivered almonds. *Serves 4.*

Calories: 320.7	Calcium: 55.4 mg.
Protein: 34.5 g.	Iron: 2.5 mg.
Fat: 9.2 g.	Sodium: 69.8 mg.
Carbohydrates: 24.8 g.	Potassium: 765.4 mg.
	Vitamin A: 398.3 IU
	Vitamin C: 43.3 mg.

SPICY INDIAN CHICKEN

In Indian cuisine, chicken is often cooked with yogurt and ghee, clarified butter. Here is a version of pungent chicken without the ghee. You can substitute peanuts, walnuts, or even pistachio nuts for cashews, although you should know that cashews have a particularly high magnesium-calcium ratio.

        ½ onion, thinly sliced
        2 tablespoons safflower oil
    1 ½ teaspoons coriander
        1 teaspoon ginger
        ½ teaspoon cardamom
        ½ teaspoon cumin
        ½ teaspoon cinnamon
        ¼ teaspoon cloves
        ¼ teaspoon red pepper flakes
        3 tablespoons unsalted, roasted cashews, chopped
        ¾ cup low-fat yogurt
        ½ cup water
        4 chicken breasts (about 2 pounds), skin removed

Sauté the onion in the oil until tender and translucent. Add the spices and nuts and simmer for 2 minutes. Stir in the yogurt and water and remove from the heat.
Preheat the oven to 350°F.
Lay the chicken breasts in a casserole. Cover with the yogurt-spice mixture and bake, covered, for 45 minutes. Let the chicken sit for at least 15 minutes before serving. *Serves 4.*

Calories: 301.5   Calcium: 71.2 mg.
Protein: 34.7 g.   Iron: 1.7 mg.
Fat: 14.4 g.   Sodium: 89.7 mg.
Carbohydrates: 6.6 g.   Potassium: 546.3 mg.
                         Vitamin A: 107.6 IU
                         Vitamin C: 2.9 mg.

CHICKEN COUSCOUS

This Moroccan stew, redolent of sweet spices and saffron, makes a meal in itself. It is filling but surprisingly light, and terrifically nutritious. It can also be made with lamb.

1 tablespoon safflower oil
1 onion, quartered
4 chicken breasts (about 1½ pounds), skin removed
6 cups Chicken Broth (page 87), or canned low-sodium broth
1 zucchini, quartered
1 yellow squash, quartered
1 white turnip, chopped
2 carrots, cut in half and quartered
1 red pepper, seeded and cut into strips
2 teaspoons cinnamon
½ teaspoon ginger
¼ teaspoon cloves
1½ teaspoons cumin
1 teaspoon turmeric
Pinch saffron
½ cup cooked chick-peas (see page 195), or use canned
¼ cup raisins
¾ cup couscous

Heat the oil in a large saucepan or soup pot and sauté the onion until translucent. Add the chicken and broth. Bring the liquid to a boil, then lower the heat and simmer for 20 minutes. Add the vegetables, spices, and chick-peas, and cook another 10 minutes, until the vegetables are soft. Stir in the raisins, cover, and keep warm. (This can be prepared a day ahead or even frozen.)

Just before serving, let the couscous soak in a bowl of 1½ cups of the cooking liquid for at least 10 minutes, until the couscous is soft. Stir frequently to break up the lumps.

When ready to serve, spread the couscous on a large platter, top with the chicken and vegetables, and spoon sauce over all. *Serves 4.*

Calories: 455.7   Calcium: 159.4 mg.
Protein: 39.9 g.   Iron: 6.2 mg.
Fat: 7.7 g.   Sodium: 309.8 mg.
Carbohydrates: 47 g.   Potassium: 1,185.9 mg.
                         Vitamin A: 10,745 IU
                         Vitamin C: 112 mg.

MUSHROOM AND
WILD RICE–STUFFED QUAIL

Quail has a rich, gamy taste that goes well with this stuffing, although you can also use it to stuff a Cornish game hen or a roast chicken or turkey. The wild rice is a good source of iron, B vitamins, and protein.

STUFFING:

1½ cups Chicken Broth (page 87), or canned low-sodium broth
½ cup wild rice
2 cloves garlic, crushed
1 shallot, minced
1 teaspoon thyme
½ teaspoon marjoram
¼ pound mushrooms, sliced

4 quail (about ½ pound each)

SAUCE:

1 cup Chicken Broth, or canned low-sodium broth
¼ cup wine
½ cup Brown Stock (page 222), or canned low-sodium beef broth

Parsley or watercress sprigs for garnish

In a large saucepan, bring 1½ cups chicken broth to a boil, then stir in the wild rice. Lower the heat until the liquid just simmers, cover, and cook for 30 minutes. Add the garlic, shallot, herbs, and mushrooms, cover, and cook another 30 minutes, or until the rice is done.

Preheat the oven to 350°F.

Stuff each quail with the wild rice mixture and place in a large roasting pan. Cover them with aluminum foil so the skins won't dry out, and bake for 1 hour, basting several times.

Bring 1 cup chicken broth and the wine to a boil in a saucepan and let the liquid reduce by half. Stir in the brown stock and keep the sauce warm.

Remove the quail, spoon some sauce over each, and serve garnished with parsley or watercress sprigs. *Serves 4.*

Calories: 508.5

Protein: 58.8 g.

Fat: 14.7 g.

Carbohydrates: 23.4 g.

Calcium: 35.7 mg.

Iron: 2.6 mg.

Sodium: 118.2 mg.

Potassium: 335.1 mg.

Vitamin A: 1,842.2 IU

Vitamin C: 7.8 mg.

ROAST TURKEY WITH
BROWN RICE, NUT, AND FRUIT DRESSING

This stuffing was the result of a Thanksgiving afternoon's joint effort on Nantucket Island and a well-stocked cupboard. At the time we used chestnuts, but they are not always easy to find, and walnuts will work equally well.

> 1 cup Chicken Broth (page 87), or canned low-sodium broth

DRESSING:
- 1½ cups brown rice
- 3 cups water
- 1 bay leaf
- 1½ tablespoons safflower oil
- 1 onion, finely chopped
- 1 stalk celery, chopped
- 1 leek, white part, chopped
- 1½ teaspoons sage
- 1 teaspoon thyme
- 2 Granny Smith apples, cored and finely chopped
- 5–6 chestnuts, roasted and chopped, or 1 ounce walnuts, chopped
- ½ cup raisins

- 1 (10–11 pound) turkey
- 1 garlic clove, crushed

Bring the water to a boil and stir in the brown rice and bay leaf. Lower the heat until the liquid simmers, cover, and cook until the rice is tender and all the liquid is absorbed, about 50 minutes to 1 hour. Discard the bay leaf.

Preheat the oven to 350°F.

Heat the oil in a large frying pan and sauté the onion, celery, and leek until soft, about 10 minutes. Add the sage, thyme, and apples and continue cooking slowly, stirring occasionally, until the apples are soft. Stir in the brown rice, raisins, and chestnuts or walnuts and keep warm.

Rinse the turkey inside and out and rub the inside cavity with the garlic clove. Stuff the turkey and bake, covered loosely with aluminum foil, for 1½ hours. Remove the foil and continue roasting for another hour, or until the leg wiggles easily.

Let the turkey sit for 15 minutes before carving. If you would like gravy, pour off the fat and reheat the natural juices with 1 cup chicken broth. *Serves 13.*

Calories: 500
Protein: 56.8 g.
Fat: 18.7 g.
Carbohydrates: 23.7 g.

Calcium: 21.2 mg.
Iron: 0.8 mg.
Sodium: 8.6 mg.
Potassium: 174.3 mg.
Vitamin A: 28.1 IU
Vitamin C: 3.9 mg.

Sixteen

Veal, Lamb, Beef

VEAL WITH
ARTICHOKES AND MUSHROOMS

Canned artichoke hearts may be substituted here if necessary, but remember that they contain a good deal of salt.

    2 artichokes
 1½ tablespoons olive oil
  ¾ pound veal scallopini, cut into bite-size pieces
  ½ pound mushrooms, sliced
    2 cloves garlic, minced
  ½ cup white wine
    2 tablespoons lemon juice
    3 tablespoons chopped parsley
    1 tablespoon chopped fresh basil, or ½ teaspoon dried
  ¼ teaspoon rosemary

Steam the artichokes until soft (about 35 to 50 minutes, depending on their size). Remove the leaves and cut out the choke. Cut the hearts into eighths and reserve.

Heat the oil in a frying pan and brown the veal. Remove and drain on paper towels.

Add the mushrooms to the pan and sauté slowly, until the mushrooms are soft and have released their liquid. Stir in the garlic and cook one minute. Add the wine, bring to a boil, and let the liquid reduce by half. Stir in the lemon juice, the herbs, the veal, and the artichoke hearts. Simmer to reheat veal and artichoke hearts, and serve. *Serves 4.*

Calories: 213.2
Protein: 20.8 g.
Fat: 10.5 g.
Carbohydrates: 12.5 g.

Calcium: 60.9 mg.
Iron: 4.4 mg.
Sodium: 118.7 mg.
Potassium: 871.7 mg.
Vitamin A: 496.1 IU
Vitamin C: 30.3 mg.

VEAL WITH MUSTARD SAUCE

2 tablespoons safflower oil
4 veal scallopini (about ¾ pound)
4 scallions, chopped
½ cup white wine
3 tablespoons Dijon or Pommery mustard
½ cup low-fat yogurt
Pepper to taste
Fresh chopped parsley or chives for garnish

Heat 1 tablespoon oil in a large frying pan and quickly sauté the veal, about 1 minute a side. Remove, drain on paper towels, and keep warm in a low oven.

Add the remaining oil to the pan and sauté the scallions until they are tender. Add the wine, increase the heat, and boil until the wine is reduced by half. Stir in the mustard, yogurt, and pepper and simmer to heat through.

Place the veal in the sauce to reheat. Serve the veal, spooning some sauce over each scallopini, and garnish with a little chopped parsley or chives. *Serves 4.*

Calories: 240.3　　　Calcium: 79.5 mg.
Protein: 19.3 g.　　　Iron: 3.1 mg.
Fat: 13.7 g.　　　　　Sodium: 387.2 mg.
Carbohydrates: 5.2 g.　Potassium: 397.1 mg.
　　　　　　　　　　　Vitamin A: 19.6 IU
　　　　　　　　　　　Vitamin C: 3.8 mg.

VEAL SCALLOPINI
WITH SAUCE DUXELLE

This recipe is adapted from a Cordon Bleu classic. The brown mushroom sauce is rich in flavor and can also be used for chicken and pasta.

SAUCE:
1½ tablespoons safflower oil
  1 onion, chopped
  1 carrot, chopped
  1 stalk celery, chopped
  1 leek, white part only, chopped
  2 cloves garlic, crushed
  1 bouquet garni:
     1 large leek leaf
     ½ teaspoon thyme
     3–4 celery leaves
     4–5 parsley sprigs
     1 bay leaf
  2 tablespoons tomato paste
¼ cup white wine
1½ cups Brown Stock (page 222), or canned low-sodium
     beef broth

¼ pound mushrooms, sliced
½ onion, finely chopped
  1 shallot, minced
2½ tablespoons safflower oil
  4 veal scallopini (about ¾ pound)

     Fresh chopped parsley for garnish

To make the sauce: In 1½ tablespoons oil, slowly sauté the onion, carrot, celery, leek, and garlic over low heat, stirring frequently until the vegetables are soft, about 10 minutes. To make the bouquet garni, fill the center of the leek leaf with thyme, celery leaves, parsley, and the bay leaf, and tie securely with string. Add the bouquet to the vegetables. Add the remaining sauce ingredients and let the liquid come to a boil. Lower the heat, cover the pan, and simmer for 30 minutes. Strain the sauce through a colander lined with cheesecloth into a bowl, pressing the vegetables to squeeze out as much liquid as possible. Return the sauce to the saucepan.

Sauté the mushrooms, onion, and shallot in 1½ tablespoons oil, cooking until most of the liquid the mushrooms give off has evaporated, about 5 minutes. Stir the mushroom mixture into the sauce and simmer for 30 minutes. The sauce should reduce and thicken.

Heat the remaining 1 tablespoon oil in a nonstick frying pan and sauté the veal quickly, about 1 minute a side, depending on its thickness. Serve the scallopini with the sauce spooned on top, and garnish with chopped fresh parsley. *Serves 4.*

Calories: 425.3   Calcium: 128.6 mg.
Protein: 25.8 g.   Iron: 6.3 mg.
Fat: 17.4 g.   Sodium: 213.6 mg.
Carbohydrates: 33.7 g.   Potassium: 1,344.6 mg.
                         Vitamin A: 10,111.5 IU
                         Vitamin C: 45.3 mg.

VEAL ROLLS WITH TOMATOES AND ZUCCHINI

Scallopini, stuffed and rolled, makes an elegant entrée. Here is an adaptation of a recipe from Cordon Bleu where the *farci,* or filling, is made with ground pork and veal. The sauce is a variation of the classic French *brunoise,* a richly flavored, burnished vegetable sauce.

4 veal scallopini (about ¾ pound)

FILLING:
1 tablespoon safflower oil
1 shallot, chopped
1 zucchini, finely chopped
1 clove garlic, minced
2 tomatoes, peeled, seeded, and chopped (see page 85)
1 tablespoon chopped fresh basil, or ½ teaspoon dried
2 tablespoons chopped fresh parsley
Chopped parsley for garnish

SAUCE:
1 onion, chopped
1 carrot, chopped
1 stalk celery, chopped
1 leek, white part only, chopped
2 cloves garlic, crushed
1½ tablespoons safflower oil
¼ cup white wine
½ cup Brown Stock (page 222), or canned low-sodium beef broth
½ cup water
1 tablespoon tomato paste
1 bouquet garni:
1 large leek leaf
½ teaspoon thyme
3–4 celery leaves
3–4 sprigs parsley
1 bay leaf

Lay the veal between sheets of waxed paper and pound until very thin.

Heat 1 tablespoon oil in a frying pan and sauté the shallot until soft. Add the zucchini and sauté until just tender, about 2 minutes. Then add the minced garlic, tomatoes, basil, and chopped parsley and cook 1 minute more.

Divide the filling between the veal pieces, laying it across the center of each scallopini. Roll up each piece of veal and tie it, like a roast, with string, making sure it is tight enough to contain the stuffing.

Preheat the oven to 325°F.

In a casserole, slowly sauté the onion, carrot, celery, leek, and crushed garlic in 1½ tablespoons oil until they are tender, about 15 minutes. Stir in the wine, brown stock, water, and tomato paste and let the liquid simmer.

Make a bouquet garni according to the directions on page 170. Add the bouquet garni to the sauce. Simmer for 15 minutes.

Place the veal in the sauce, cover the casserole, and bake for 25 minutes. Remove the veal and carefully cut off the string. Strain the sauce through a colander lined with cheesecloth, pressing hard on the vegetables to squeeze out the liquid. Reheat the sauce and spoon it over the veal rolls. Serve garnished with chopped parsley. *Serves 4.*

Calories: 345.4	Calcium: 119.1 mg.
Protein: 23.2 g.	Iron: 5.5 mg.
Fat: 14.6 g.	Sodium: 148.8 mg.
Carbohydrates: 27.5 g.	Potassium: 1,238.6 mg.
	Vitamin A: 7,334.8 IU
	Vitamin C: 65.9 mg.

VEAL CHOPS WITH BASIL SAUCE

Basil—particularly fresh basil—gives veal a refreshing taste. This sauce also can be used with veal scallopini or lamb chops.

2 tablespoons safflower oil
4 rib veal chops (about 1½ pounds)
1 shallot, finely chopped
2 cloves garlic, minced
½ cup white wine
½ cup Brown Stock (page 222), or canned low-sodium beef broth
4 tablespoons chopped fresh basil, or 1½ teaspoons dried

Preheat the oven to 325°F.

In a large frying pan, heat 1 tablespoon oil and brown the veal chops on both sides. Remove and place in a large casserole.

Heat the remaining tablespoon of oil in a saucepan and sauté the shallot until soft. Add the garlic and wine, bring the liquid to a boil, and let it reduce by half. Stir in the brown stock and basil, pour the sauce over the chops, cover the frying pan, and bake for 30 minutes.

Remove the chops. Strain the sauce through a colander lined with cheesecloth. Reheat the sauce and spoon it over the chops. *Serves 4.*

Calories: 340.8   Calcium: 47.4 mg.
Protein: 27.1 g.   Iron: 4.8 mg.
Fat: 18.8 g.   Sodium: 155.2 mg.
Carbohydrates: 8.1 g.   Potassium: 662.9 mg.
                            Vitamin A: 2,228.5 IU
                            Vitamin C: 19.4 mg.

STUFFED VEAL ROAST

Because veal has very little fat it should be cooked in a covered casserole or covered with aluminum foil, so that it doesn't dry out.
Loins and rumps are usually best for roasts; however, you can also
use a 3-pound breast of veal, which is a less-expensive cut.

STUFFING:
½ pound spinach
½ onion, chopped
1 tablespoon safflower oil
½ cup whole-wheat bread crumbs
1 beaten egg
2 ounces walnuts, chopped
¼ teaspoon thyme

1 (2-pound) loin or rump of veal, boned and rolled

SAUCE:
2 tablespoons safflower oil
1 onion, chopped
2 carrots, chopped
2 leeks, white part only, chopped
1 stalk celery, chopped
3 cloves garlic, crushed
4 cups Brown Stock (page 222), or canned low-sodium
   beef broth
1 bouquet garni:
   1 large leek leaf
   ½ teaspoon thyme
   3–4 celery leaves
   3–4 sprigs parsley
   1 bay leaf

Preheat the oven to 350°F.
Wash the spinach well and cook it for 2 to 3 minutes in boiling water, until it is just wilted. Drain in a colander and rinse with
cold water. Drain well, then, taking small clumps, squeeze out the
excess water with your hands. Drain on paper towels and chop.
Sauté ½ chopped onion in 1 tablespoon oil until soft. Combine

the onion with the spinach, bread crumbs, egg, walnuts, and thyme. Make a deep incision into the veal, and stuff with the spinach mixture. Sew up the opening with string.

Heat 2 tablespoons safflower oil in a large roasting pan and sauté 1 chopped onion, the carrots, the leeks, and the celery until soft. Add the garlic and brown stock. Make a bouquet garni according to the directions on page 170 and add it to the sauce. Place the veal on top of the vegetables and bring the liquid to a boil. Cover the veal with aluminum foil and bake, basting several times, for 1¾ hours.

Remove the veal and strain the sauce through a colander lined with cheesecloth into a bowl, pressing as much liquid as possible out of the vegetables. Slice the veal, and serve it with the sauce on the side. *Serves 4.*

Calories: 594.2   Calcium: 204.5 mg.
Protein: 43.5 g.   Iron: 9.8 mg.
Fat: 25.6 g.   Sodium: 380.7 mg.
Carbohydrates: 47.7 g.   Potassium: 1,660.2 mg.
                           Vitamin A: 15,066.6 IU
                           Vitamin C: 66.1 mg.

BLANQUETTE DE VEAU

This recipe is adapted from the classic French veal stew, of which it is a rich but lower-calorie version. As with all stews, its flavor improves if it is made a day before serving.

    2 pounds stew veal, cut into 1½-inch pieces
    1 bouquet garni:
        1 large green leek leaf
        ½ teaspoon thyme
        3–4 parsley sprigs
        3–4 celery leaves
        1 bay leaf
    5 cups Chicken Broth (page 87), or canned low-sodium
      broth
    1 large onion, studded with 4 cloves
    2 carrots, peeled and cut in half
   12 white onions, peeled
    2 tablespoons margarine
    2 tablespoons flour
 1½ tablespoons fresh lemon juice
      White pepper
   12 ounces mushrooms, cleaned and quartered
      Chopped fresh parsley for garnish

In a large stew pot, poach the veal in 3 to 4 cups water for 2 minutes. Strain well, rinse off the scum from the veal, and clean out the pot.

Make a bouquet garni by filling the leek leaf with the thyme, parsley, celery leaves, and bay leaf. Roll up the herbs in the leaf, like a cigarette, and tie it shut with string.

Return the veal to the pot and add the chicken broth, onion studded with cloves, carrots, and bouquet garni. Bring the liquid to a boil, then simmer, covered, for 1 hour.

Strain the veal, reserving the liquid.

While the veal is cooking, cook 12 onions in a large saucepan of water until soft, about 20 minutes. Strain.

In another saucepan, melt the margarine, then stir in the flour and cook, stirring, over a low heat for 2 to 3 minutes, to cook out the flour taste. Remove the pan from the heat and pour in the hot reserved veal stock. Return the pan to the heat and, whisking constantly, cook until the sauce thickens. Stir in the lemon juice and pepper. Lower the heat, add the mushrooms, and simmer for 15 to 20 minutes, until they are tender.

Return the veal to the pot with the onions. Stir in the mushrooms and sauce, and reheat, or refrigerate and serve the next day. Serve with egg noodles or long-grain and wild rice, sprinkled with parsley. *Serves 6.*

Calories: 405.3
Protein: 38.2 g.
Fat: 14 g.
Carbohydrates: 25.5 g.

Calcium: 98.1 mg.
Iron: 7.4 mg.
Sodium: 340.8 mg.
Potassium: 1,107.6 mg.
Vitamin A: 5,564.5 IU
Vitamin C: 25 mg.

GRILLED BUTTERFLIED
LEG OF LAMB

The rich flavor of lamb lends itself to several herbs, but of course mint is a popular favorite. If herbs de provence is not available, substitute a teaspoon of rosemary and a little thyme.

> 1 (4½-pound) boned and butterflied leg of lamb (about 7½ pounds with bone)

MARINADE:
3 cloves garlic, crushed
3 tablespoons olive oil
2 tablespoons lemon juice
4 tablespoons chopped fresh mint
1 tablespoon herbs de provence
1 bay leaf, crushed
  Pepper to taste
  Fresh watercress sprigs for garnish

Trim the fat from the lamb and put it in a baking dish or pan.

Mix the marinade ingredients together, pour over the lamb, cover with plastic wrap, and marinate for at least 6 hours at room temperature, or overnight in the refrigerator.

Scrape off the herbs and grill the lamb over a charcoal fire or under the broiler. If you're using a broiler, cook the lamb for 10 to 15 minutes a side for rare (depending on the thickness of the lamb and how high it is above the flame) and about 18 to 22 minutes a side for medium. If you're using a grill, place the rack several inches away from the flame. (Cooking time will be about the same, but with both, check the lamb before turning.)

Let the lamb sit for at least 15 minutes before serving. Slice into thin pieces, and serve garnished with watercress. *Serves 12.*

Calories: 329.3	Calcium: 17.8 mg.
Protein: 25.8 g.	Iron: 2.3 mg.
Fat: 24.1 g.	Sodium: 128.6 mg.
Carbohydrates: 0.7 g.	Potassium: 598.6 mg.
	Vitamin A: 128.8 IU
	Vitamin C: 3.6 mg.

LEMON-ROASTED LEG OF LAMB

A variation on the traditional lemon-and-garlic-scented lamb, this further heightens the meat's flavor with mustard and rosemary.

    1 (7-pound) leg of lamb
    2 cloves garlic, sliced
    ¼ onion, minced
    ¼ cup lemon juice
    1 tablespoon Dijon mustard
    ½ teaspoon rosemary
      Pepper to taste

Preheat the oven to 300°F.

Trim the fat off the lamb. Make several slits in the meat and insert the garlic. Mix the remaining ingredients in a small bowl and pour over the lamb. Cook, basting frequently, about 1 hour and 40 minutes for rare, 2 hours and 20 minutes for medium. (The internal temperature on a meat thermometer will be about 150° for rare, 160° for medium.) Let the lamb sit 15 minutes before carving. *Serves 10.*

    Calories: 323.7   Calcium: 21 mg.
    Protein: 27.7 g.   Iron: 2.3 mg.
    Fat: 22.3 g.   Sodium: 176 mg.
    Carbohydrates: 1.4 g.   Potassium: 77.7 mg.
                             Vitamin A: 3.1 IU
                             Vitamin C: 3.2 mg.

GINGERED LAMB MEATBALLS

MEATBALLS:
- ¾ pound ground lamb
- 2 cloves garlic, minced
- ¼ onion, minced
- 2 slices whole-wheat or cracked-wheat bread
- 4 tablespoons finely chopped fresh parsley
- ½ egg, beaten
- 3 tablespoons toasted pine nuts, ground
- 1½ tablespoons grated fresh ginger
- Pepper to taste

- 2 tablespoons safflower oil

SAUCE:
- 1 tablespoon safflower oil
- ½ cup minced onion
- 1 (28-ounce) can tomato purée
- 1 tablespoon tomato paste
- 2 cloves garlic, minced
- ½ teaspoon cinnamon

In a large bowl, mix together all the ingredients for the meatballs. Shape the mixture into 1½-inch balls.

Heat 2 tablespoons oil in a large frying pan. Cook the meatballs, one layer at a time, over low heat until they are done, about 2 minutes per side. Drain on paper towels and keep warm.

Heat 1 tablespoon oil in a saucepan and sauté ½ cup minced onion until it is golden brown. Add the remaining sauce ingredients, lower the heat, and simmer for 15 minutes. When ready to serve, carefully stir in the meatballs and reheat them for a few minutes in the sauce. Serve over brown rice, kasha, or pasta. *Serves 4.*

Calories: 378.2
Protein: 25.8 g.
Fat: 18.9 g.
Carbohydrates: 29.8 g.

Calcium: 68.2 mg.
Iron: 6.2 mg.
Sodium: 144.6 mg.
Potassium: 1,626.3 mg.
Vitamin A: 3,926.2 IU
Vitamin C: 80.2 mg.

NAVARIN OF LAMB

Navarin of lamb, a delicate French lamb stew, is often prepared with tender spring vegetables. Here is a version made with fresh herbs as well. The basics of the stew can be prepared a day ahead; then, just before serving, add the fresh vegetables and remaining ingredients.

1½ pounds lamb shoulder, cut into 1½- to 2-inch pieces, or 2 pounds lamb shanks or neck with bone
  6 cups water
  2 garlic cloves, crushed
  6 carrots, quartered
  1 onion, quartered
  1 leek, white part only, chopped
  1 stalk celery, sliced
  2 tablespoons chopped fresh basil
  1 bouquet garni:
    1 large leek leaf
    ½ teaspoon thyme
    3–4 celery leaves
    3–4 parsley sprigs
    1 bay leaf
10 white onions
  1 pound peas
  ½ pound green beans
  ½ cup white wine
  3 tablespoons tomato paste

Put the lamb in a large saucepan or soup pot with the water, the garlic, 2 carrots, 1 onion, and the leek, celery, and basil. Make a bouquet garni according to the directions on page 170. Add the bouquet garni to the pot, bring the liquid to a boil, then lower the heat, cover the pot, and simmer gently for 1½ hours.

Remove the meat and strain the liquid through a colander lined with cheesecloth, discarding the vegetables and bouquet garni. Clean out the pot and add the lamb with the strained broth, 4 carrots, and 10 onions. Let the stew simmer for 15 minutes, then add the peas and beans. Stir in the wine and tomato paste and simmer until the vegetables are tender. (If the broth is too thin, thicken by mixing 2 to 3 tablespoons cornstarch with ¼ cup water, stir until smooth, then whisk into the stew and cook, stirring several times, until it thickens.) *Serves 5.*

Calories: 492.2   Calcium: 157.7 mg.
Protein: 25.5 g.   Iron: 5.2 mg.
Fat: 26 g.   Sodium: 177.4 mg.
Carbohydrates: 38.3 g.   Potassium: 1,444.1 mg.
                            Vitamin A: 20,356.8 IU
                            Vitamin C: 62 mg.

BOILED BEEF
WITH HORSERADISH SAUCE

A variation of the classic French pot-au-feu, this simple stew was often served as Sunday dinner when I was a child, with a rich, fiery horseradish sauce. I've substituted a quieter sauce and added leeks to the stew to enhance the flavor.

      1 (3–3½-pound) rump or chuck roast
      4 carrots, quartered
      2 onions, quartered
      2 leeks, white part, sliced in half
      1 stalk celery, cut into chunks
      ½ yellow turnip, peeled and quartered
      1 bouquet garni:
        1 large leek leaf
        ½ teaspoon thyme
        3–4 celery leaves
        3–4 sprigs parsley
        1 bay leaf
    5–6 peppercorns

VEGETABLES:
      3 carrots, quartered
    6–8 white onions, peeled
      2 leeks, white part only, cut in half
      2 white turnips, peeled and quartered
      ½ pound green beans

SAUCE:
      1 cup low-fat yogurt
    2–3 tablespoons horseradish
      2 tablespoons lemon juice
      ¼ teaspoon white pepper

Tie up the roast so that it won't fall apart as it cooks. Place the roast in a large soup pot with 4 carrots, 2 onions, 2 leeks, the celery, and yellow turnip. Add enough water to cover the meat by 2 inches.

Make a bouquet garni according to the directions on page 170.

Add the bouquet garni and the peppercorns to the soup pot.

Bring the liquid to a boil, lower the heat, and simmer, covered, for about 2 hours. Remove the carrots, onions, leeks, turnip, and celery, and add 3 fresh carrots, 6 to 8 onions, 2 leeks, and the white turnips. Cover and simmer for another 20 to 30 minutes. Add the green beans and continue cooking until they are tender.

Combine the yogurt, horseradish, lemon juice, and pepper in a bowl. Carve the meat into thin slices, and serve with the vegetables and horseradish sauce. *Serves 8.*

Calories: 532.8	Calcium: 190.3 mg.
Protein: 32 g.	Iron: 6.3 mg.
Fat: 31.5 g.	Sodium: 194.7 mg.
Carbohydrates: 31.7 g.	Potassium: 1,399.9 mg.
	Vitamin A: 14,138.5 IU
	Vitamin C: 46.9 mg.

MEAT LOAF WITH
SPINACH AND MOZZARELLA

I have added spinach (for iron), cheese (for calcium), and wheat germ (for iron and B vitamins) to the traditional meat loaf recipe. The result is a rich and delicious dish, which improves in flavor if it sits for a day or two.

½ pound spinach
1 pound lean ground round
2 shallots, finely chopped
2 cloves garlic, minced
1 tablespoon Dijon mustard
2 teaspoons Worcestershire
1 tablespoon horseradish
1 egg
2 pieces whole-wheat bread
3 tablespoons wheat germ
2 tablespoons tomato paste, or 3 tablespoons Brown Stock
   (page 222) or canned low-sodium beef broth
2 tablespoons chopped fresh parsley
½ cup grated skim-milk mozzarella (2 ounces)
1 tablespoon grated Parmesan

Preheat the oven to 400°F.

Wash the spinach well. In a large saucepan, bring 1 cup water to a boil, add the spinach, and cook until it is just wilted. Rinse under cold water and drain well in a colander. When it is cool enough to handle, take clumps of spinach in your hands and squeeze out any excess water. Dry on paper towels, and chop.

In a large bowl, combine the beef, shallots, garlic, mustard, Worcestershire, horseradish, and egg. Rip the bread into small pieces and process them in a blender or food processor until they are crumbs. Add them with the wheat germ, tomato paste or brown stock, and parsley to the beef and mix well.

Make a large, flat oval shape with half the meat mixture; lay it in a small roasting pan. Press down in the center to make a well, leaving ½-inch border around the edges. Fill the well with spinach, then the cheeses. Cover the filling with the remaining meat mixture, pressing down to seal the edges. Bake for 40 minutes. *Serves 5.*

Calories: 313.9   Calcium: 224.9 mg.
Protein: 33.1 g.   Iron: 7.5 mg.
Fat: 11.4 g.   Sodium: 399.5 mg.
Carbohydrates: 20.9 g.   Potassium: 1,091.5 mg.
                             Vitamin A: 3,516.9 IU
                             Vitamin C: 34.4 mg.

BEEF STEW EN DAUBE

The base of this classic country stew of Provence is marinated beef,
vegetables, and wine. This version uses less fat in the cooking and
adds brown stock for more flavor. If you'd like, add 2 tablespoons of
Cognac with the marinade as well.

¾ pound lean stew beef, cut in 1-inch cubes
1 cup red wine
3 cloves garlic, minced
1 shallot, finely chopped
3 carrots, quartered
2 onions, quartered
¼ teaspoon rosemary
½ teaspoon thyme
   Pepper to taste
1 bay leaf
1½ tablespoons safflower oil
1 tablespoon flour
½ cup Brown Stock (page 222), or canned low-sodium
   beef broth
½ cup water
½ cup fresh peas
½ pound mushrooms, quartered

In a large bowl, mix the beef with the wine, garlic, shallot, carrots, onions, rosemary, thyme, pepper, and bay leaf. Cover with plastic wrap and marinate at room temperature for at least 3 hours, or in
the refrigerator for 6 hours. Strain through a colander, reserving the
liquid.
Preheat the oven to 350°F.
In a large saucepan, heat the oil and brown the meat. Sprinkle
the flour over the meat and stir to coat well. Add ¼ cup reserved
marinade, the brown stock, and the water, stir to mix well, cover,
and bake for 1½ hours.
Remove the saucepan, add the peas and mushrooms, and cook
30 minutes more, until all the vegetables are tender. *Serves 4.*

Calories: 428   Calcium: 111.5 mg.
Protein: 25.2 g.   Iron: 5.6 mg.
Fat: 16.7 g.   Sodium: 145.9 mg.
Carbohydrates: 34.9 g.   Potassium: 1,247 mg.
                               Vitamin A: 13,852.8 IU
                               Vitamin C: 32.5 mg.

Seventeen

Pastas and Grains

PASTA WITH ZUCCHINI, CARROTS, AND BASIL

This is a light, colorful pasta recipe that goes well with lamb, chicken, or fish. It is high in vitamin A and is a rich source of calcium and fiber.

    4 carrots
    2 zucchini
    ½ pound fresh or dried egg or spinach linguine
    3 tablespoons chopped fresh basil, or 1½ teaspoons dried
    1 tablespoon chopped fresh parsley

Finely julienne the carrots and zucchini so they resemble strands of linguine. Steam them until just tender, about 2 minutes.

Cook the linguine in boiling water for 1 minute, or until it is *al dente*. Drain. Toss with the vegetables, basil, and parsley, and serve. *Serves 4.*

Calories: 222   Calcium: 83.4 mg.
Protein: 8.5 g.   Iron: 2.6 mg.
Fat: 0.9 g.   Sodium: 42.3 mg.
Carbohydrates: 46.1 g. Potassium: 556 mg.
                       Vitamin A: 13,185 IU
                       Vitamin C: 29.8 mg

PASTA WITH SQUASH, TOMATOES, AND WALNUTS

Walnuts lend this colorful sauce a surprising texture as well as a calcium and iron boost, and squash provides a generous dose of potassium. This is one of my favorite sauces for pasta; be sure to serve it immediately, however, so the squash does not get soggy.

1 small acorn squash
1 tablespoon safflower oil
¼ onion, chopped
3 tomatoes, peeled, seeded, and chopped (see page 85)
1 clove garlic, minced
3 tablespoons chopped fresh parsley
1 tablespoon lemon juice
2 ounces walnuts, chopped
½ pound fresh or dried linguine or fettuccine

Cut the squash in half, scrape out the seeds, cut off the skin, and cut into small chunks. Steam the squash a few minutes, until it just begins to get soft. While the squash is steaming, bring a large pot of water to a boil.

Heat the oil in a saucepan and sauté the onion until it is soft. Stir in the tomatoes and cook for 1 minute. Add the squash, garlic, parsley, and lemon juice and cook just to reheat the squash. Stir in the nuts. Cover and remove from the heat.

Cook the pasta in boiling water until it is just *al dente* (about 1 minute for fresh linguine, 2 to 3 for fresh fettuccine). Drain, and served topped with the sauce. *Serves 4.*

Calories: 418.4   Calcium: 92.8 mg.
Protein: 12.8 g.   Iron: 4.1 mg.
Fat: 13.3 g.   Sodium: 10.2 mg.
Carbohydrates: 66 g.   Potassium: 1,083.9 mg.
                           Vitamin A: 2,564 mg.
                           Vitamin C: 55.6 mg.

PASTA WITH HERBED TOMATO SAUCE

This sauce makes a delicious substitute for standard tomato sauce and is rich in calcium, iron, and vitamins A and C.

> 2 tablespoons safflower oil
> 1 bunch scallions, chopped
> 5 tomatoes, peeled, seeded, and chopped (see page 85), or
>   1 14½-ounce can low-sodium tomatoes, well drained
> 2 tablespoons tomato paste
> ¾ cup chopped fresh parsley
> ¼ cup chopped fresh dill
> ½ pound fresh or dried linguine or fettuccine
>   Grated Parmesan cheese (optional)

Heat the oil in a large saucepan and sauté the scallions until soft. Add the tomatoes, tomato paste, parsley, and dill, mix well, and simmer gently for 30 minutes.

Bring 1 quart of water to a boil and cook the pasta until it is *al dente* (about 1 minute for fresh linguine, 2 to 3 minutes for fresh fettuccine). Drain well, and serve topped with the sauce and a little grated Parmesan, if desired. *Serves 4.*

Calories: 350.4   Calcium: 70.9 mg.
Protein: 10.9 g.   Iron: 3.9 mg.
Fat: 8.1 g.   Sodium: 18.6 mg.
Carbohydrates: 60 g. Potassium: 961.7 mg.
                     Vitamin A: 2,621.3 IU
                     Vitamin C: 78.7 mg.

PASTA PRIMAVERA

Pasta primavera is usually made with a cream sauce. Here is one made with pesto that can be served hot or cold.

    1 bunch broccoli (about 1 pound)
    1 pound green beans
    2 red peppers, seeded and cut into strips
    1 zucchini, chopped
   ¾ pound spinach, tomato, or whole-wheat fusilli (pasta twists)
 1½ cups Pesto (page 221)
      Grated Parmesan cheese (optional)

Separate the broccoli into flowerets. (Reserve the stems for soup.) Cut the beans in half. Steam the beans for 2 minutes, add the broccoli and peppers, and steam another 5 to 7 minutes, until the broccoli just begins to feel tender. Add the zucchini and steam 2 to 3 minutes more, until just tender. Remove the vegetables and keep warm.

Cook the pasta in boiling water until it is just *al dente.* Drain well; toss in a large bowl with the vegetables and Pesto. Serve hot with a little grated Parmesan, or cold as a salad. *Serves 7.*

Calories: 354.8	Calcium: 136.1 mg.
Protein: 13.1 g.	Iron: 3.5 mg.
Fat: 12.5 g.	Sodium: 18.6 mg.
Carbohydrates: 51.2 g.	Potassium: 671.3 mg.
	Vitamin A: 4,982.9 IU
	Vitamin C: 172.2 mg.

PASTA WITH BROCCOLI SAUCE

This is a terrific, light sauce loaded with calcium and vita-min C.

1 head broccoli (about 1 pound)
4 cloves garlic, minced
1 tablespoon olive oil
1 tablespoon safflower oil
½ pound fresh or dried spinach or egg linguine or fettucine

Separate the broccoli into flowerets and steam until just tender.

Quickly sauté the garlic in the oils, then add the broccoli, stir-ring to coat with garlic. Remove from the heat and keep warm while you cook the pasta.

Bring 1 quart of water to a boil and cook the pasta as directed if it's dried. (If it's fresh, about 1 minute for linguine, 2 to 3 minutes for fettucine.) Drain and serve on a large platter or individual plates, topped with the broccoli. *Serves 4.*

Calories: 306
Protein: 10.7 g.
Fat: 7.7 g.
Carbohydrates: 49.8 g.

Calcium: 108 mg.
Iron: 2,7 mg.
Sodium; 15.6 mg.
Potassium: 482.8 mg.
Vitamin A: 2,210 IU
Vitamin C: 100.9 mg.

HERBED SPINACH LASAGNA

Here is a lighter version of lasagna made with fresh herbs and vegetables in place of meat. Make it a day or two before serving, as the flavor improves over time.

SAUCE:
1½ tablespoons safflower oil
 1 large onion, finely chopped
 ¾ pound mushrooms, sliced
 4 cloves garlic, minced
 2 (28-ounce) cans tomato purée, without salt
 6 tablespoons chopped fresh basil, or 3 teaspoons dried
 6 tablespoons chopped fresh parlsey
 3 tablespoons chopped fresh dill, or 1½ teaspoons dried
1½ teaspoons oregano
 Pepper to taste
 1 zucchini, chopped

 2 pounds spinach
 ¾ pound lasagna
1½ cups low-fat cottage cheese
 12 ounces skim-milk ricotta
 8 ounces skim-milk mozzarella, grated

Heat the oil in a large saucepan and sauté the onion, stirring frequently, until tender and translucent. Add the mushrooms and sauté until they are soft. Add the garlic, tomato purée, and herbs and simmer for 30 minutes. Stir in the zucchini and simmer another 10 minutes.

Preheat the oven to 350° F.

While the sauce is simmering, bring 1 cup water to a boil in a large pot. Stir in the spinach and cook until it is just wilted. Drain the spinach well in a colander and rinse with cold water until it is cool enough to handle. Press out as much water as possible with a wooden spoon. Then take small clumps of spinach in your hands and squeeze out the remaining water. Drain the spinach on paper towels, then chop.

Bring 1 quart of water to a boil and cook the lasagna until it is *al dente* (about 10 minutes). Drain through a colander, rinsing with cold water until it is cool enough to handle.

Assemble the lasagna in a 9-by-13-inch lasagna dish. Spread a little sauce across the bottom of the pan. Then make a layer with half the lasagna. Spread half the cottage cheese and ricotta carefully across the lasagna. Sprinkle half the spinach over the cheeses. Cover the spinach with half the remaining sauce, then with half the mozzarella. Make a second layer with the remaining ingredients.

Bake the lasagna for 30 minutes. Let sit for 10 minutes before serving. *Serves 15.*

Calories: 252.9

Protein: 44.8 g.

Fat: 4.6 g.

Carbohydrates: 34.1 g.

Calcium: 258.9 mg.

Iron: 5.2 mg.

Sodium: 244.7 mg.

Potassium: 1,009.8 mg.

Vitamin A: 5,854 IU

Vitamin C: 78.2 mg.

SWEET INDIAN RICE

Brown rice is an ideal source of B vitamins, especially niacin (B_3).
Serve this rice as a side dish with chicken or lamb or with Cauliflower Curry (page 205). It is quite sweet and very spicy.

  ¾ cup brown rice
2¼ cups Chicken Broth (page 87), or canned low-sodium
     broth
  1 onion, quartered and sliced
  2 cloves garlic, crushed
  ⅛ teaspoon ginger
  ½ teaspoon cinnamon
  ¼ teaspoon cardamom
  ⅛ teaspoon ground cloves
  2 tablespoons roasted, unsalted cashews, chopped
  ¼ cup raisins
  1 tablespoon grated fresh ginger

Combine the rice, broth, and spices in a saucepan, bring the liquid to a boil, then lower the heat and simmer, covered, for 45 minutes, or until the rice is tender and all the liquid is absorbed. (Add a
little more broth, if needed.)

Remove the garlic, stir in the cashews, raisins, and fresh ginger,
and serve. *Serves 4.*

Calories: 208.2   Calcium: 39.1 mg.
Protein: 6.3 g.   Iron: 2 mg.
Fat: 3.0 g.   Sodium: 83.9 mg.
Carbohydrates: 36.4 g. Potassium: 255.3 mg.
                  Vitamin A: 29 IU
                  Vitamin C: 5.9 mg.

BROWN RICE
WITH PARSLEY-NUT SAUCE

This recipe was inspired by a Middle Eastern dish, *gormeh sabzee,* an unforgettable lamb stew that contains 6 cups of parsley. Parsley is very high in vitamins A and C; the walnuts here add iron and fiber, as well as crunch.

  2¼ cups Chicken Broth (page 87), or canned low-sodium
      broth
   ¾ cup brown rice
    1 tablespoon safflower oil
    4 scallions, chopped
    1 clove garlic, minced
   ¾ cup chopped fresh parsley
    2 ounces walnuts, chopped

In a saucepan, bring the chicken broth to a boil and stir in the rice. Lower the heat and simmer for 45 minutes to 1 hour, until the liquid is absorbed and the rice is tender.

In another saucepan, heat the oil and sauté the scallions until they are tender. Add the garlic, parsley, and walnuts and cook another minute. Stir the sauce into the rice. *Serves 4 as a side dish.*

Calories: 263.1   Calcium: 44 mg.
Protein: 6.6 g.   Iron: 1.9 mg.
Fat: 12.8 g.   Sodium: 78.2 mg.
Carbohydrates: 27.7 g.   Potassium: 269.1 mg.
                         Vitamin A: 322.8 IU
                         Vitamin C: 10.5 mg.

BROWN RICE AND VEGETABLES

The ubiquitous food of the sixties, brown rice is now recognized as a more nutritious (and tastier) alternative to its white counterpart. If the bitter taste does not bother you, try kale in place of spinach here—it's a much better source of calcium. And, if salt intake is not a problem for you, add a little soy sauce.

    2 cups water
    ¾ cup brown rice
    1 bay leaf
    ¼ pound spinach or kale
    1 onion, quartered
    2 carrots, quartered and sliced
    ½ pound broccoli, cut into flowerets
    ¼ head cabbage or bok choy, quartered and thickly sliced
    1 white turnip, quartered and thinly sliced
    3 tablespoons grated fresh ginger
    1 large clove garlic, minced
    1 tablespoon safflower oil
    1 tablespoon sesame oil
    3 tablespoons toasted sesame seeds

Bring the water to a boil, stir in the rice and bay leaf, lower the heat, and simmer, covered, until the rice is tender and the liquid is absorbed, about 45 minutes. Keep warm.

In a large saucepan, cook the spinach in boiling water until just tender, about 2 minutes. If you're using kale, boil it for 10 minutes. (This reduces the bitterness.) Drain well, squeezing out the excess water with the back of a spoon.

In another large saucepan, steam the onion, carrots, broccoli, cabbage, and turnip until just tender.

Heat the oils and sauté the ginger and garlic for 30 seconds, stirring constantly. Add the vegetables and toss well. Spoon the rice onto a platter or 4 plates, and top with the vegetables. Sprinkle the vegetables with the sesame seeds, and serve. *Serves 4.*

Calories: 315.2   Calcium: 266.8 mg.
Protein: 9.4 g.   Iron: 4.4 mg.
Fat: 11.7 g.   Sodium: 111.1 mg.
Carbohydrates: 47.3 g.   Potassium: 1,685.9 mg.
                         Vitamin A: 11,173.7 IU
                         Vitamin C: 106.9 mg.

BULGUR CASSEROLE

Bulgur, the cracked kernels of dried wheat, is available in health-food stores and some supermarkets. This can be served as an entrée or, in smaller portions, as a side dish. It is a fine source of calcium, iron, potassium, and B vitamins.

> 1½ cups bulgur
> 1 tablespoon safflower oil
> 1 onion, chopped
> 1 green pepper, chopped
> ¼ pound mushrooms, sliced
> 3 tomatoes, peeled, seeded, and chopped (page 85)
> 2 cloves garlic, minced
> ½ teaspoon oregano
> 2 tablespoons chopped fresh basil, or 1 teaspoon dried
> 1 cup low-fat cottage cheese

Soak the bulgur in 3 cups water for 30 minutes, until soft. Drain well, and reserve.

Heat the oil in a frying pan and sauté the onion and pepper until tender, about 5 minutes. Add the mushrooms and cook until they are soft. Add the tomatoes, garlic, and herbs and cook another 2 minutes.

Stir in the bulgur and let it reheat. Just before serving, add the cottage cheese and cook until warm. *Serves 4.*

Calories: 353.8	Calcium: 108.1 mg.
Protein: 16.8 g.	Iron: 4.5 mg.
Fat: 5.1 g.	Sodium: 171.9 mg.
Carbohydrates: 62 g.	Potassium: 862.9 mg.
	Vitamin A: 1,189.5 IU
	Vitamin C: 99.9 mg.

BULGUR WITH CHICK-PEAS

The combination of bulgur and chick-peas makes the protein in this dish complete. This makes a fine entrée with a salad, and it's high in B vitamins, calcium, and iron.

½ cup chick-peas
1 cup bulgur
1 tablespoon safflower oil
1 onion, chopped
1 zucchini, finely chopped
3 tomatoes, peeled, seeded, and chopped (page 85)
1 clove garlic, minced
2 tablespoons lemon juice
2 tablespoons chopped fresh parsley
½ teaspoon marjoram
¼ teaspoon rosemary

Soak the chick-peas in water several hours or overnight. Drain and rinse in a colander, then cook in a pot of simmering water for 1 hour, or until they are tender. Drain.

Let the bulgur soak in a bowl in 3 cups water, then drain well.

Heat the oil in a saucepan and sauté the onion until it is tender and translucent. Add the zucchini and cook, stirring frequently, until soft. Then add the tomatoes, garlic, lemon juice, and herbs and cook 2 more minutes. Stir in the chick-peas and bulgur and simmer 10 minutes. *Serves 4.*

Calories: 300.6.
Protein: 11.2 g.
Fat: 5.2 g.
Carbohydrates: 55.9 g.

Calcium: 98.2 mg.
Iron: 4 mg.
Sodium: 17.5 mg.
Potassium: 869.1 mg.
Vitamin A: 501.5 IU
Vitamin C: 57.9 mg.

*VEGETARIAN COUSCOUS**

This is a meatless adaptation of the North African favorite. It makes a fine side dish with fish, chicken, lamb, or veal, and can be served cold as a salad. It is high in vitamins A and C and is a good source of fiber.

    ¾ cups couscous
  1½ cups Chicken Broth (page 87), or canned low-sodium
        broth
    ½ onion, finely chopped
    1 zucchini, diced
    2 carrots, diced
    ½ red pepper, diced
    ½ teaspoon cinnamon
    ¼ teaspoon ginger
    ⅛ teaspoon cloves
    ½ teaspoon cumin
    ½ teaspoon turmeric
        Pinch of saffron

Heat the chicken broth and pour it over the couscous. Mix well and let the couscous stand until it is fluffy and the liquid has been absorbed, about 10 minutes. (You'll need to stir it a few times with a fork to break up any lumps.)

At the same time, steam the vegetables in a large, covered saucepan until just tender, about 2 minutes. Mix the vegetables with the couscous. Add the spices and mix well. Serve immediately, or chill and serve in tomato cups. *Serves 4.*

Calories: 112.6   Calcium: 61.1 mg.
Protein: 5 g.   Iron: 1.5 mg.
Fat: 0.4 g.   Sodium: 86.6 mg.
Carbohydrates: 21.1 g.   Potassium: 405 mg.
                         Vitamin A: 9,441.7 IU
                         Vitamin C: 52.8 mg.

---

* Iron, sodium, potassium, and vitamin A values for the couscous grain are not available; figures include all other ingredients.

LENTIL AND VEGETABLE STEW

A good winter stew not only high in calcium, iron, potassium, vitamin A, and the B vitamins, but low in calories and fat.

- ¾ cup lentils
- ½ onion, chopped
- 1 white turnip, chopped
- 1 leek, white part only, chopped
- 3 carrots, quartered and sliced
- ½ pound green beans, diced
- 1 bay leaf
- 3 cups Chicken Broth (page 87), or canned low-sodium broth
- 1 zucchini, quartered and sliced
- ¼ pound spinach, shredded
- 1½ teaspoons dried basil
- ½ teaspoon thyme

Rinse the lentils in a colander and drain. Put the lentils in a large saucepan with the onion, turnip, leek, carrots, beans, bay leaf, and chicken broth. Let the broth come to a boil, then lower the heat and simmer, covered, for 20 minutes.

Add the zucchini, spinach, basil, and thyme, cover, and simmer another 10 minutes. Remove the bay leaf and serve in large soup bowls. *Serves 4.*

Calories: 173.2
Protein: 9.8 g.
Fat: 0.8 g.
Carbohydrates: 28.7 g.

Calcium: 163 mg.
Iron: 4.4 mg.
Sodium: 179.2 mg.
Potassium: 927.6 mg.
Vitamin A: 13,983.7 IU
Vitamin C: 60.4 mg.

MILLET WITH
CARROTS, ZUCCHINI, AND MINT

Millet is one of my favorite grains—it has a hearty, cornlike taste that goes well with many vegetables. Nutritionally, it is one of the best sources of iron and has no sodium; it also has one of the highest magnesium-calcium ratios among the grains. You can find it in most health-food stores.

    1 cup millet
    2 carrots, diced
    1 zucchini, diced
    4 scallions, chopped
    4 tablespoons chopped fresh mint, or 2 teaspoons dried
    2 tablespoons chopped fresh parsley
    3 tablespoons fresh lemon juice

Heat an iron skillet and roast the millet, stirring frequently, until it begins to brown, about 5 to 6 minutes. Put the millet in a saucepan with 2 cups water and simmer, covered, for 30 minutes. Drain well.

Combine the millet with the vegetables, mint, parsley, and lemon juice. Serve warm, or cold as a salad. *Serves 4.*

Calories: 215.5   Calcium: 72.7 mg.
Protein: 7.1 g.   Iron: 4.7 mg.
Fat: 1.2 g.   Sodium: 37.5 mg.
Carbohydrates: 48.4 g.   Potassium: 672.5 mg.
                      Vitamin A: 9,002.2 IU
                      Vitamin C: 34.9 mg.

WINTER CASSEROLE

This casserole comes from a vegetarian friend in the Berkshires. Both the soybeans and rice are high in B vitamins; the combination makes the protein content of this recipe complete. As with most casseroles, this one's flavor improves if it sits for a day or two.

¼ cup dry soybeans
1 bay leaf
¾ cup brown rice
1 onion, chopped
1 tablespoon safflower oil
2 cloves garlic, minced
2 tablespoons chopped fresh basil, or ¼ teaspoon dried
½ teaspoon oregano
6 tomatoes, peeled, seeded, and chopped (page 85)
2 tablespoons tomato paste
1 large zucchini, chopped
Low-fat cottage cheese (optional)

Soak the soybeans overnight. Bring 2 to 3 cups water to a boil, add the soybeans and bay leaf, lower the heat, and simmer, covered, for 3 hours, until tender, adding more water if needed. Drain the soybeans, reserving the water for the rice. Discard the bay leaf.

Bring 2¼ cups water to a boil (use the soybean water, adding more water if needed), add the rice, lower the heat, and simmer, covered, until the rice is tender and the liquid is absorbed, about 45 minutes to 1 hour.

In a large saucepan, heat the oil and sauté the onion until tender and translucent. Add the remaining ingredients and simmer until the zucchini is tender. Stir in the rice and soybeans and reheat. Serve with a little low-fat cottage cheese. *Serves 4.*

Calories: 244.6   Calcium: 81.4 mg.
Protein: 7.8 g.   Iron: 3 mg.
Fat: 5.1 g.   Sodium: 22.4 mg.
Carbohydrates: 44.8 g.   Potassium: 929.4 mg.
                         Vitamin A: 2,334.7 IU
                         Vitamin C: 76.4 mg.

ENCHILADAS WITH BEAN FILLING

Enchiladas can be made with a variety of fillings. Here is one which—with its kidney-bean filling—provides large amounts of protein, calcium, and iron. Enchiladas filled with steamed vegetables, spinach, or chicken are also delicious.

BEAN FILLING:
   1 tablespoon corn oil
   ½ onion, finely chopped
   ½ green pepper, seeded and finely chopped
   2 cloves garlic, minced
   2 cups cooked kidney beans

   3 cups Enchilada Sauce (page 219)
   8 corn tortillas
   4 ounces part-skim cheese, such as mozzarella, grated

Heat the oil in a frying pan and sauté the onion and pepper until soft. Add the garlic and beans and cook for 5 minutes. (You can mash the beans if you'd like, or purée them in a food processor or blender.)

Preheat the oven to 350° F. Spoon a little sauce into the bottom of a casserole.

Heat a small iron frying pan. Heat the tortillas, one at a time, until soft, then spoon a little filling down the center. Roll the enchilada and place it in the casserole. Repeat with the remaining tortillas. Cover the enchiladas with the remaining sauce, sprinkle the cheese on top, and bake for 30 minutes. *Serves 4.*

Calories: 411.2   Calcium: 279.9 mg.
Protein: 19.8 g.   Iron: 5.2 mg.
Fat: 16.5 g.   Sodium: 125.7 mg.
Carbohydrates: 53 g.   Potassium: 1,068.8 mg.
                       Vitamin A: 2,737.6 IU
                       Vitamin C: 104 mg.

Eighteen

Vegetables

CARROTS WITH
ONION AND PARSLEY

Loaded with vitamin A and high in fiber, carrots lend themselves to a variety of interesting flavor combinations. Try them also with fresh basil or mint.

> ½ onion, chopped
> 1 tablespoon margarine
> 2 tablespoons water
> 3 carrots, julienned
> 3 tablespoons chopped fresh parsley

In a large saucepan, sauté the onion in the margarine. Add the water and the carrots, cover, and steam until the carrots are tender, about 2 minutes. Stir in the parsley and serve. *Serves 5.*

Calories: 76.2   Calcium: 51.8 mg.
Protein: 1.6 g.   Iron: 1.0 mg.
Fat: 3.6 g.   Sodium: 82.2 mg.
Carbohydrates: 10.6 g. Potassium: 315.9 mg.
                        Vitamin A: 12,248.3 IU
                        Vitamin C: 17.4 mg.

BROCCOLI AND CAULIFLOWER BOWL

This simple and stunning dish comes from Kathy Melo, who owns the Company of the Cauldron restaurant on Nantucket Island.

½ pound broccoli
1 head cauliflower
2 tablespoons lemon juice
1 tablespoon safflower oil

Separate the broccoli and cauliflower into flowerets, trying to make them as uniform in size as possible. (Save the stems for soup.) Steam the vegetables until just tender, then sprinkle them with lemon juice.

Lightly oil a large bowl. Alternate pieces of broccoli and cauliflower, laying them in the bowl so that the flowerets are against the side and the stems face inward. Make sure to pack the vegetables tightly. Cover the bowl and keep warm until ready to serve.

Just before serving, invert the bowl on a platter and carefully remove the bowl. (If any of the pieces seem loose, push them back in.) *Serves 6.*

Calories: 47   Calcium: 56.7 mg.
Protein: 2.8 g.   Iron: 0.95 mg.
Fat: 2.49 g.   Sodium: 12.7 mg.
Carbohydrates: 5.2 g.   Potassium: 270.8 mg.
                                    Vitamin A: 1,132.5 IU
                                    Vitamin C: 86 mg.

VEGETABLE KEBABS

Try these kebabs with Grilled Butterflied Leg of Lamb (page 172), Orange Chicken (page 150), or any grilled meat, poultry, or fish.

½ pound white onions
1 yellow squash (about ¾ pound)
1 zucchini (about ¾ pound)
¾ pound mushrooms
1 green pepper
1 red pepper
1 pound cherry tomatoes

MARINADE:
⅛ cup safflower oil
⅛ cup olive oil
¼ cup lemon juice
½ cup orange juice
1 tablespoon Dijon mustard
3 cloves garlic, crushed
3 tablespoons chopped fresh basil, or 1½ teaspoons dried
3 tablespoons chopped fresh parsley
½ teaspoon marjoram

Steam the onions until they just begin to feel tender, about 10 minutes. Remove from the heat and reserve.

Cut the squash and zucchini into thick slices. Remove the stems from the mushrooms. Remove the seeds from the peppers and cut them into 1½- to 2-inch cubes.

Mix the marinade ingredients together well. In a large bowl, mix the vegetables and toss with the marinade. Cover with plastic wrap and refrigerate for several hours.

On 4 skewers, alternate pieces of each vegetable. Cook the kebabs over a grill until just tender, about 15 minutes, turning a few times so they don't burn. *Serves 8.*

Calories: 130.5   Calcium: 56.7 mg.
Protein: 4.2 g.   Iron: 1.7 mg.
Fat: 7 g.   Sodium: 64.2 mg.
Carbohydrates: 13.5 g.   Potassium: 609.3 mg.
                         Vitamin A: 2,029 IU
                         Vitamin C: 180.9 mg.

CARROTS WITH CARDAMOM

Orange and cardamom are an excellent combination and make perfect companions for carrots.

¾ cup fresh orange juice
4 carrots, sliced
½ onion, chopped
½ teaspoon cardamom

Bring the orange juice to a boil and add the carrots, onion, and cardamom. Lower the heat and simmer, covered, until the carrots are tender, about 7 minutes, adding more orange juice if needed. *Serves 5.*

Calories: 60.5
Protein: 1.7 g.
Fat: 0.3 g.
Carbohydrates: 13.8 g.

Calcium: 48.8 mg.
Iron: 0.8 mg.
Sodium: 41.9 mg.
Potassium: 364.8 mg.
Vitamin A: 12,674 IU
Vitamin C: 25.7 mg.

CAULIFLOWER CURRY

This recipe came about when I was experimenting with different curries; I have always liked the taste of cauliflower and curry and added the peas for a touch of color and fiber. Serve this over brown rice for a light dinner.

  1 head cauliflower
  ½ onion, chopped
  ½ pound fresh peas, shelled
  ½ teaspoon cinnamon
  ¼ teaspoon cloves
  1 clove garlic, minced
  1 tablespoon grated fresh ginger
  ½ teaspoon turmeric
  ½ teaspoon cumin
    Dash cayenne
  ¼ teaspoon fenugreek
  2 cups Chicken Broth (page 87), or canned low-sodium broth
  ¾ cup low-fat yogurt
    Sesame seeds or chopped cashews for garnish (optional)

Separate the cauliflower into flowerets and place them in a large saucepan with the onion, peas, spices, and chicken broth. Let the broth come to a boil, then lower the heat and simmer, covered, for 10 minutes.

Remove the saucepan from the heat. Stir in the yogurt until it is thoroughly blended, then reheat. Serve the curry over rice, or as a side dish, garnished, if desired, with a few sesame seeds or chopped cashews. *Serves 4.*

Calories: 93.6   Calcium: 86.2 mg.
Protein: 6.9 g.   Iron: 1.9 mg.
Fat: 1.1 g.   Sodium: 98.5 mg.
Carbohydrates: 11.4 g.   Potassium: 322.7 g.
                            Vitamin A: 218.2 IU
                            Vitamin C: 60.8 mg.

SUMMER CASSEROLE

Zucchini, summer tomatoes, and fresh basil make for a fine combination. If good tomatoes are not available, you can use low-salt canned tomatoes or tomato sauce.

2 zucchini, sliced
3 tomatoes, peeled and thinly sliced
1 onion, thinly sliced
4 tablespoons chopped fresh basil, or 2 teaspoons dried
1 large clove garlic, minced
2 tablespoons chopped fresh parsley
   Freshly ground pepper to taste
   Chopped fresh parsley or grated Parmesan for garnish

Preheat the oven to 325° F.

Lightly oil the bottom of a casserole with vegetable oil. Make a layer of zucchini, then tomatoes, then onions. Sprinkle half the basil, garlic, and parsley over the onions, then repeat with the remaining ingredients. Cover the casserole and bake for 30 minutes. Serve sprinkled with a little chopped parsley or Parmesan. *Serves 4.*

Calories: 76   Calcium: 77.6 mg.
Protein: 4.1 g.   Iron: 1.9 mg.
Fat: 0.5 g.   Sodium: 13.8 mg.
Carbohydrates: 16.5 g.   Potassium: 721.5 mg.
                                 Vitamin A: 1,915.9 IU
                                 Vitamin C: 71.4 mg.

RATATOUILLE

Traditionally, ratatouille is simmered for a long period of time in quite a lot of oil. Here is a recipe without most of the oil and, consequently, the calories. This casserole gets better as it sits, so make it a day or two ahead.

　1　tablespoon safflower oil
　1　tablespoon olive oil
　½　onion, chopped
　1　green pepper, seeded and cut in strips
　1　red pepper, seeded and cut in strips
　1　small eggplant, cubed
　2　zucchini, cubed
　3　large cloves garlic, minced
　3　tomatoes, peeled, seeded, and chopped (page 85)
　2　tablespoons tomato paste
　3　tablespoons chopped fresh basil, or 1½ teaspoons dried
　1　teaspoon oregano
　　　Pepper to taste
　　　Grated Parmesan and chopped parsley for garnish
　　　(optional)

Heat the oils in a large saucepan and sauté the onions and peppers, stirring frequently, until they are soft. Add the eggplant, zucchini, and garlic. Cook the vegetables for 15 minutes over a low heat, stirring frequently so they don't burn.

Add the tomatoes and tomato paste. Stir in the basil, oregano, and pepper to taste, cover, and simmer for 1 hour. Serve with a little grated Parmesan and chopped parsley, as a sauce for pasta, or as an omelette filling. *Serves 8.*

Calories: 90　　　　　　Calcium: 42.4 mg.
Protein: 3.1 g.　　　　Iron: 1.6 mg.
Fat: 3.8 g.　　　　　　Sodium: 11.9 mg.
Carbohydrates: 13.2 g.　Potassium: 500.2 mg.
　　　　　　　　　　　Vitamin A: 2,203.5 IU
　　　　　　　　　　　Vitamin C: 100.6 mg.

STUFFED ZUCCHINI

Serve this zucchini dish with a salad as an entrée. This filling also works well in eggplant or tomato shells. The mushrooms are a good source of zinc and the sunflower seeds are high in iron and calcium.

        2 zucchini (about 1½ pounds)
     1½ tablespoons safflower oil
        3 scallions, chopped
       ¼ pound mushrooms, chopped
        1 cup cooked brown rice
        1 large clove garlic, minced
        4 tablespoons chopped fresh parsley
       ¼ teaspoon marjoram
       ½ teaspoon thyme
        2 ounces roasted sunflower seeds
       ½ cup low-fat cottage cheese
       ¼ cup grated Fontina or Jarlsberg cheese

Preheat the oven to 300° F.

Slice the zucchini lengthwise and scoop out the insides, leaving a ¼-inch shell. Chop the scooped-out insides of the zucchini.

Heat the oil and sauté the scallions and mushrooms, stirring frequently. Cook until the mushrooms have released their liquid, about 2 minutes. Add the chopped zucchini and continue to cook until the liquid has evaporated.

Mix the rice, garlic, parsley, herbs, sunflower seeds, cottage cheese, and walnuts with the zucchini-mushroom mixture. Fill the zucchini shells and sprinkle the tops with grated cheese. Place the shells in a lightly oiled roasting pan and bake, covered with foil, for 25 minutes. Remove the foil, turn up the heat to 400° F., and bake another 10 minutes. *Serves 4.*

Calories: 256.8   Calcium: 163.6 mg.
Protein: 12.8 g.   Iron: 2.6 mg.
Fat: 13.9 g.   Sodium: 277.6 mg.
Carbohydrates: 23.1 g.   Potassium: 760.5 mg.
                           Vitamin A: 984.9 IU
                           Vitamin C: 42.3 mg.

COUSCOUS-STUFFED TOMATOES

Tomato shells make perfect cases, warm or cold, for a variety of salads or vegetables. Try this also with Millet with Carrots, Zucchini, and Mint (page 198) or Lentil Salad (page 108).

    4 large, ripe tomatoes
    ½ recipe Vegetarian Couscous (page 196)
       Lettuce
       Sliced cucumbers
       Watercress

Cut off the tops of the tomatoes, then scoop out the centers with the seeds, leaving the sides intact. If the tomatoes don't stand on their own, level the bottom by taking off a small slice. Turn the tomatoes over onto paper towels and let them drain for at least 15 minutes.

Preheat the oven to 350° F.

Fill the shells with couscous. Lightly oil the bottom of a small roasting pan. Put the shells in the pan, cover with aluminum foil, and bake for 25 minutes.

If you'd like to serve these as a salad, fill the cups and chill until ready to serve. Serve on a bed of lettuce, garnished with thinly sliced cucumbers and watercress. *Serves 4.*

    Calories: 100.3   Calcium: 56.5 mg.
    Protein: 4.7   Iron: 1.7 mg.
    Fat: 0.6 g.   Sodium: 49.3 mg.
    Carbohydrates: 19.9 g.   Potassium: 689.5 mg.
                             Vitamin A: 6,015.8 IU
                             Vitamin C: 71.4 mg.

VEGETARIAN CHILI

I prefer this chili to one with meat. It's lighter, with less calories, fat, and protein. Kidney beans are rich in calcium and iron. Make this chili a day before serving to allow the flavors time to meld.

    1 cup kidney beans
    1 tablespoon safflower oil
    1 onion, chopped
    2 cloves garlic, minced
    4 tomatoes, peeled, seeded, and chopped (page 85)
    1 cup tomato juice
    1 tablespoon tomato paste
    1 teaspoon cumin
    2 teaspoons chili powder
    2 tablespoons chopped fresh basil, or ½ teaspoon dried
    1 zucchini, sliced
      Part-skim cheese and chopped parsley for garnish
      (optional)

In a large saucepan, bring 3 cups of water to a boil and add the beans. Lower the heat until the water simmers and cook the beans, covered, for 1 hour, or until they are soft. Drain and reserve.

Heat the oil in a large saucepan and sauté the onion until soft and translucent. Add the garlic, tomatoes, tomato juice, tomato paste, and herbs and simmer for 30 minutes.

Stir in the kidney beans and the zucchini and simmer for 10 minutes, or until the zucchini is tender. Serve over brown rice or sprinkled with a little part-skim cheese and parsley. *Serves 4.*

    Calories: 183.9   Calcium: 80.9 mg.
    Protein: 8.3 g.   Iron: 3.3 mg.
    Fat: 4.3 g.   Sodium: 92.2 mg.
    Carbohydrates: 30.6 g.   Potassium: 1172.8 mg.
                             Vitamin A: 2,076.3 IU
                             Vitamin C: 71.2 mg.

EGGPLANT PARMESAN

Eggplant need not be sautéed in oil, as most Parmesan recipes suggest. If you slice the eggplant thinly and bake it for an hour, it will emerge perfectly tender and extremely flavorful. Eggplant should also be prepared this way to accompany Herbed Tomato Sauce (page 186). This recipe provides much calcium and iron, and the mushrooms are high in zinc.

    1 eggplant (about 1 pound)
    8 ounces skim-milk mozzarella, grated
    1 tablespoon grated Parmesan

SAUCE:
    1 tablespoon safflower oil
    1 onion, chopped
    ¼ pound mushrooms, chopped
    2 cloves garlic, minced
    ½ teaspoon oregano
    4 tablespoons fresh basil or 2 teaspoons dried
    1 (28-ounce) can tomato purée (low-sodium)

Preheat the oven to 350° F.

Heat the oil in a saucepan and sauté the onion until soft. Add the mushrooms and continue cooking until they are tender. Add the garlic, oregano, basil, and tomato purée, and simmer for 15 minutes.

Cut the eggplant into thin slices. Lightly oil the bottom of a casserole. Place a layer of eggplant on the bottom and top with sauce, then with half the mozzarella. Repeat with the remaining ingredients and sprinkle the Parmesan over the top. Cover and bake for 45 minutes, or until the eggplant is tender. *Serves 4.*

Calories: 335.9   Calcium: 551.3 mg.
Protein: 21.1 g.   Iron: 4.9 mg.
Fat: 17 g.   Sodium: 257.9 mg.
Carbohydrates: 30.4 g.   Potassium: 1,458.7 mg.
                         Vitamin A: 3,806.7 IU
                         Vitamin C: 76.3 mg.

SPICED SQUASH

Of the winter squashes, buttercup has a natural sweetness that needs little flavoring or sweetening. However, butternut or acorn squash can also be used. This squash makes a terrific Thanksgiving side dish.

2 buttercup, butternut, or acorn squash (about 2 pounds)
½ teaspoon allspice
¼ teaspoon cloves

Prick the squash several times with a fork or knife and bake at 350° F. for 1 hour, or until tender. Remove the squash, cut in half, and scrape out the seeds. Scoop the squash into a saucepan and stir in the spices. Just before serving, mash well with a fork and reheat. *Serves 4.*

Calories: 85.5   Calcium: 51 mg.
Protein: 2.2 g.   Iron: 1.3 mg.
Fat: 0.2 g.   Sodium: 1.5 mg.
Carbohydrates: 22.2 g.   Potassium: 773 mg.
                          Vitamin A: 9,050 IU
                          Vitamin C: 14.5 mg.

MILLET-STUFFED GREEN PEPPERS

Brown rice, bulgur, or lentils can be substituted for millet, but I prefer the taste of millet, which happens to have one of the best magnesium-calcium ratios among the grains. It is also a low-fat source of iron and protein. This recipe is high in vitamin A, and the broccoli and cottage cheese give it plenty of calcium.

   4 green peppers
   ½ onion, chopped
   ½ pound broccoli, separated into small flowerets
   1 red pepper, seeded and chopped
   1 cup cooked millet (see page 198)
   ¾ cup low-fat cottage cheese
   4 tablespoons chopped fresh parsley
   ½ teaspoon oregano
   3 tablespoons chopped fresh basil, or 1½ teaspoons dried
   ½ cup Basic Tomato Sauce (page 219), or canned
      low-sodium tomato sauce, or Herbed Tomato Sauce
      (page 186)

Preheat the oven to 350° F.

Remove the stems and seeds from the green peppers. Rinse them out and drain well on paper towels. (If they can't stand on their own, cut off a thin, even slice from the bottom.)

Steam the onion, broccoli, and red pepper until just tender, about 3 to 4 minutes. Mix the vegetables in a bowl with the millet, cottage cheese, parsley, oregano, and basil. Fill the peppers with the mixture. Top each with a little tomato sauce, and bake for 25 to 30 minutes, until the peppers are soft. *Serves 4.*

   Calories: 288.4   Calcium: 138.5 mg.
   Protein: 15.7 g.   Iron: 6.6 mg.
   Fat: 2 g.   Sodium: 151 mg.
   Carbohydrates: 57.8 g.   Potassium: 902.7 mg.
                            Vitamin A: 4,944.3 IU
                            Vitamin C: 373.2 mg.

DILL NEW POTATOES

    8 new potatoes (about 1½ pounds)
    4 sprigs fresh dill
    1 tablespoon margarine
    3 tablespoons chopped fresh dill
      Freshly ground pepper to taste

In a large saucepan, steam the potatoes with the dill sprigs until tender, about 15 to 20 minutes. Melt the margarine in another pan and add the chopped dill and potatoes, stirring just to coat. Season with freshly ground pepper. *Serves 4.*

Calories: 136   Calcium: 17.4 mg.
Protein: 3.1 g.   Iron: 1.1 mg.
Fat: 3.5 g.   Sodium: 46.7 mg.
Carbohydrates: 23.8 g. Potassium: 586.3 mg.
                     Vitamin A: 427.3 IU
                     Vitamin C: 33.2 mg.

MEXICAN POTATOES

Here is a piquant recipe that can be used as a side dish or as a filling for enchiladas, and which will prove that potatoes do not need butter or salt to make them palatable. I seldom skin potatoes because the skins can be quite tasty and they contain many nutrients.

    1 pound potatoes
    1 tablespoon corn or safflower oil
    ½ onion, chopped
    ½ green pepper, seeded and chopped
    1½ teaspoons chili powder
    ½ teaspoon cumin
        Freshly ground pepper to taste

Wash the potatoes well and cut them into small cubes. Steam them until tender, about 10 minutes.

In a frying pan, heat the oil and sauté the onion and green pepper until tender, stirring frequently. Add the potatoes and spices and mix well. Season to taste with freshly ground pepper. *Serves 4.*

Calories: 114.5   Calcium: 15.4 mg.
Protein: 2.5 g.   Iron: 0.8 mg.
Fat: 3.5 g.   Sodium: 8.3 mg.
Carbohydrates: 19 g.   Potassium: 451.3 mg.
                       Vitamin A: 106.3 IU
                       Vitamin C: 50.5 mg.

Nineteen

Sauces and Dressings

DILL SAUCE

Try this sauce cold in seafood salads or with cold poached salmon. It can also be heated and served with poached fish, fish soufflé, or steamed vegetables. If you can't find fresh dill, you can use 1½ teaspoons dried.

> 1 cup low-fat yogurt
> 1 (8-ounce) cake tofu
> 4 tablespoons fresh dill
> 3 tablespoons lemon juice
> ½ teaspoon pepper

Purée all the ingredients in a blender or food processor. *Makes 2 cups.*

Per 2 tablespoons: Calcium: 29.9 mg.
Calories: 14.5   Iron: 0.3 mg.
Protein: 1.3 g.   Sodium: 7.1 mg.
Fat: 0.7 g.   Potassium: 29.5 mg.
Carbohydrates: 3.5 g.   Vitamin A: 85.2 IU
    Vitamin C: 2.4 mg.

BASIC TOMATO SAUCE

You can use any herb in this sauce; basil, oregano, and dill are always good, but you may want to try sage or chervil instead. If good summer tomatoes are not available, substitute canned, unsalted plum tomatoes.

½ onion, or 2 shallots, chopped
½ tablespoon safflower oil
2 tomatoes (about 1 pound)
1 clove garlic
2 tablespoons chopped fresh basil or dill, or ½ teaspoon dried herbs such as basil, dill, oregano, chervil, or sage
Freshly ground pepper to taste

Peel, seed, and chop the tomatoes, according to directions on page 85.

Heat the oil in a saucepan and sauté the onion or shallots until soft and translucent. Add the tomatoes, garlic, and herbs, reduce the heat, and simmer, covered, for 20 minutes.

Purée the sauce in a food processor or blender. Scrape the sauce back into the saucepan and season with freshly ground pepper. *Makes 1¾ cups.*

Per ½ cup: Calcium: 23.2 mg.
Calories: 55.8   Iron: 0.8 mg.
Protein: 1.8 g.   Sodium: 6.6 mg.
Fat: 2.2 g.   Potassium: 334 mg.
Carbohydrates: 8.4 g. Vitamin A: 751.4 IU
                      Vitamin C: 28.8 mg.

MARINARA SAUCE

Serve this sauce with pasta or try it with chicken, fish, or shrimp.

> 6–8 plum tomatoes (about 1½ pounds)
> 1 tablespoon olive oil
> 2 shallots, minced
> 2 cloves garlic, minced
> 4 tablespoons tomato paste
> 1 teaspoon oregano
> ¼ teaspoon rosemary
> 4 tablespoons chopped fresh parsley
> Pepper to taste

Peel, seed, and finely chop the tomatoes according to directions on page 85.

Heat the oil in a large saucepan and sauté the shallots until tender. Add the tomatoes, garlic, tomato paste, herbs, and pepper to taste. Cover and simmer for about 30 minutes. *Makes about 3½ cups.*

Per ½ cup:
Calories: 62
Protein: 2.1 g.
Fat: 2.2 g.
Carbohydrates: 9.6 g.

Calcium: 25.4 mg.
Iron: 1.4 mg.
Sodium: 12.6 mg.
Potassium: 443.2 mg.
Vitamin A: 1,435.8 IU
Vitamin C: 36.8 mg.

ENCHILADA SAUCE

Be sure to wear rubber gloves when handling jalapeño peppers, or remember to wash your hands carefully afterward. If you can find fresh coriander, use it (about 1 tablespoon); otherwise, dried works fine.

1 tablespoon safflower oil
½ onion, finely chopped
1 can unsalted crushed tomatoes
2 jalapeño peppers, seeded and finely chopped
2 cloves garlic, minced
½ teaspoon coriander

Heat the oil in a large saucepan and sauté the onion until tender and translucent. Add the remaining ingredients, cover, and simmer for about 30 minutes. *Makes about 4 cups.*

Per ½ cup:
Calories: 58.5
Protein: 1.2 g.
Fat: 1.7 g.
Carbohydrates: 8.8 g.

Calcium: 5.6 mg.
Iron: 1.8 mg.
Sodium: 7.5 mg.
Potassium: 451.2 mg.
Vitamin A: 1,622 IU
Vitamin C: 44.7 mg.

MINTED VEGETABLE SAUCE

This simple puréed vegetable sauce goes well with fish, poultry, or Spinach Soufflé Roll (page 114).

¼ pound snow peas
1½ cups fresh peas
3 scallions, chopped
1 cup Chicken Broth (page 87), or low-sodium canned broth
3 tablespoons fresh mint, or 1 teaspoon dried
¼ cup low-fat yogurt

Cut the stems off the snow peas and peel off the strings. Place all ingredients in a saucepan except the mint and yogurt, bring the broth to a boil, then simmer for 15 minutes. Add the mint.

Purée the mixture in a food processor or blender. Return the sauce to the pan, stir in the yogurt, and reheat. Serve immediately, or refrigerate for up to 5 days. *Makes about 1½ cups.*

Per ¼ cup:
Calories: 47.2
Protein: 3.3 g.
Fat: 1 g.
Carbohydrates: 7.2 g.
Calcium: 38.8 mg.
Iron: 1.1 mg.
Sodium: 27.9 mg.
Potassium: 135.6 mg.
Vitamin A: 482.8 IU
Vitamin C: 15.5 mg.

PESTO

Here is a pesto that calls for less oil and consequently makes for a thicker, more pungent sauce. Add a little to vinaigrettes, mayonnaise, even tuna salads.

2 cloves garlic
3 cups fresh basil leaves, tightly packed
1 cup fresh parsley
½ teaspoon pepper
4 tablespoons olive oil
3 tablespoons safflower oil
3 ounces pine nuts

In a food processor or blender, purée the garlic, basil, parsley, and pepper. Then, with the machine running slowly, add the oil. (If you're using a blender pour in a little oil, purée the mixture, then add a little more oil, continuing until you have a smooth paste.) Add the pine nuts and process until they are finely chopped. *Makes 1½ cups.*

Per 2 tablespoons: Calcium: 11.2 mg.
Calories: 55.9   Iron: 0.3 mg.
Protein: 1.4 g.   Sodium: 2.7 mg.
Fat: 5.3 g.   Potassium: 84.7 mg.
Carbohydrates: 1.2 g. Vitamin A: 453.4 IU
                      Vitamin C: 9.9 mg.

BROWN STOCK

One of the flavor bases for French sauces is *fond de veau,* a concentrated, rich veal stock that greatly enhances many meat or poultry entrées. *Fond de veau,* or brown stock, is traditionally made by browning veal bones and vegetables. This gives the stock its reddish-brown color and releases the marrow that gels the stock. This recipe is a simpler version, using gelatin instead of veal bones.

Because brown stock is essential to so many recipes and because it keeps for months in the freezer, I recommend doubling or tripling this recipe.

2 tablespoons safflower oil
2 onions, chopped
3 carrots, chopped
2 stalks celery, chopped
2 leeks, white part only, chopped
1 bouquet garni:
  1 large leek leaf
  ½ teaspoon thyme
  3–4 celery leaves
  3–4 sprigs parsley
  1 bay leaf
4 cups Chicken Broth (page 87), or canned low-sodium broth
½ cup white wine
3 cloves garlic, crushed
3 tomatoes, peeled, seeded, and chopped (page 85)
3 tablespoons tomato paste
1 envelope gelatin

Heat the oil in a large saucepan or soup pot and sauté the onions, carrots, celery, and leeks slowly until they are tender, about 15 minutes.

While the vegetables are cooking, make the bouquet garni according to the directions on page 170. Add the broth, wine, garlic, tomatoes, tomato paste, and bouquet garni to the vegetables, bring the liquid to a boil, then lower the heat and simmer, covered, for 30 to 45 minutes.

Strain the stock through a colander lined with cheesecloth into a large bowl, pressing all the liquid out of the vegetables with the back of a spoon. Return the stock to the pot, stir in the gelatin, and cook slowly for a few minutes. Use the stock immediately, or refrigerate for up to one week, or freeze for up to three months. *Makes about 3½ cups.*

Per ½ cup:
Calories: 155.4
Protein: 6.6 g.
Fat: 2.4 g.
Carbohydrates: 17.9 g.

Calcium: 73.6 mg.
Iron: 2.4 mg.
Sodium: 122.1 mg.
Potassium: 551.5 mg.
Vitamin A: 7,368.7 IU
Vitamin C: 25.3 mg.

SIMPLE VINAIGRETTE

¼ cup tarragon or wine vinegar
½ clove garlic, minced
 1 teaspoon Dijon mustard
¼ teaspoon freshly ground pepper
⅓ cup olive oil

Mix the vinegar, garlic, mustard, and pepper in a bowl. Whisk in the oil until it is thoroughly blended, or mix the dressing in a blender. *Makes about ¾ cup.*

Per 1 tablespoon:
Calories: 36.6
Protein: 0.05 g.
Fat: 4 g.
Carbohydrates: 0.3 g.

Calcium: 0.9 mg.
Iron: .02 mg.
Sodium: 8.8 mg.
Potassium: 2.4 mg.
Vitamin A: trace
Vitamin C: 0.03 mg.

HERB VINAIGRETTE

¼ cup tarragon or wine vinegar
2 tablespoons fresh lemon juice
Pepper to taste
1 clove garlic, minced
1 scallion, finely chopped
2 tablespoons chopped fresh dill or basil or 1 teaspoon
dried, or ½ teaspoon oregano, or ¼ teaspoon tarragon
¼ cup olive oil
¼ cup safflower oil

Mix the vinegar, lemon juice, pepper, garlic, scallion, and herbs in a bowl. Whisk in the oil slowly, stirring until it is thoroughly blended. *Makes about 1 cup.*

Per 1 tablespoon: Calcium: 0.44 mg.
Calories: 45.6   Iron: 0.01 mg.
Protein: 0.03 g.   Sodium: 0.3 mg.
Fat: 5 g.   Potassium: 5.1 mg.
Carbohydrates: 0.36 g.   Vitamin A: 0.02 IU
                           Vitamin C: 0.7 mg.

LEMON-MUSTARD DRESSING

¼ cup fresh lemon juice
1 tablespoon Dijon mustard
¼ cup olive oil
¼ cup safflower oil
Pepper to taste

In a small bowl, mix the lemon juice and mustard. Whisk in the oils until they are thoroughly blended, or mix all the ingredients in a blender. Add pepper to taste. *Makes ¾ cup.*

Per 1 tablespoon:
Calories: 61.5
Protein: 0.13 g.
Fat: 6.8 g.
Carbohydrates: 0.2 g.

Calcium: 2.7 mg.
Iron: .04 mg.
Sodium: 26.2 mg.
Potassium: 6.8 mg.
Vitamin A: 0.6 IU
Vitamin C: 1.4 mg.

TOFU MAYONNAISE

Here, at last, is a mayonnaise high in protein, calcium, and iron and low in fat and calories. Use it instead of regular mayonnaise, or add herbs and try it as a salad dressing.

>   1 (8-ounce) cake tofu
>   ½ cup water
>   4 tablespoons wine or tarragon vinegar
>   2 tablespoons olive oil

In a blender or food processor, purée all the ingredients. *Makes 1 cup.*

Per 2 tablespoons:	Calcium: 29.1 mg.
Calories: 40.6	Iron: 0.4 mg.
Protein: 1.7 g.	Sodium: 1.6 mg.
Fat: 3.6 g.	Potassium: 10.1 mg.
Carbohydrates: 5.6 g.	Vitamin A: 0
	Vitamin C: 0

CURRY-YOGURT DRESSING

    1 cup low-fat yogurt
    ¼ cup Apple-Peach Chutney (page 230)
    1 teaspoon curry or to taste

    Mix all ingredients in a bowl. Let sit for 30 minutes before using. *Makes 1¼ cups.* Use with Curried Chicken Salad (page 106), any tossed greens, or raw vegetable salad.

Per 2 tablespoons:	Calcium: 29.7 mg.
Calories: 24.9	Iron: 0.1 mg.
Protein: 0.9 g.	Sodium: 12.4 mg.
Fat: 0.4 g.	Potassium: 53.9 mg.
Carbohydrates: 4.5 g.	Vitamin A: 84.4 IU
	Vitamin C: 1 mg.

LUE CHEESE DRESSING

with tossed greens or over sliced fresh tomatoes and

   1 cup low-fat yogurt
1½ ounces finely crumbled blue cheese
     Pepper to taste

Mix all ingredients together well. *Makes 1 cup.*

Per 2 tablespoons: Calcium: 49.4 mg.
Calories: 32.4   Iron: .03 mg.
Protein: 2 g.   Sodium: 14.3 mg.
Fat: 2 g.   Potassium: 40 mg.
Carbohydrates: 1.5 g. Vitamin A: 81.6 IU
                       Vitamin C: 0.3 mg.

APPLE-PEACH CHUTNEY

        1 pound peaches, peeled, pitted, and chopped
        1 pound Granny Smith apples, peeled, cored, and chopped
        1 cup cider vinegar
       ½ cup brown sugar
        1 cup apple juice
        1 onion, chopped
       ¼ cup raisins
        3 garlic cloves, minced
        2 teaspoons ginger
      2½ teaspoons cinnamon
       ½ teaspoon cloves
        1 teaspoon allspice
        1 teaspoon dry mustard
        2 tablespoons crystallized ginger, finely chopped

Mix all the ingredients in a saucepan, bring the liquid to a simmer, cover, and cook for 30 minutes. Remove the chutney from the heat and let it cool. Store in sterilized jars in the refrigerator. *Makes about 4 cups.*

Per 2 tablespoons: Calcium: 14.4 mg.
Calories: 65.3   Iron: 0.6 mg.
Protein: 0.5 g.   Sodium: 4.2 mg.
Fat: 0.1 g.   Potassium: 109.9 mg.
Carbohydrates: 16.9 g. Vitamin A: 343.5 IU
                        Vitamin C: 3.9 mg.

RASPBERRY SAUCE

Serve this sauce on fresh fruit, with Lemon Mousse (page 235), or in plain yogurt.

   1 pint raspberries
   2 tablespoons *framboise* (raspberry liqueur) or Grand Marnier
   3 tablespoons chopped fresh mint
   1 tablespoon lemon juice

   Purée all the ingredients in a blender or food processor. *Makes about 2 cups.*

   Per ¼ cup: Calcium: 11.7 mg.
   Calories: 25.2   Iron: 0.4 mg.
   Protein: 0.5 g.   Sodium: 1.3 mg.
   Fat: 0.2 g.   Potassium: 76.9 mg.
   Carbohydrates: 5.4 g.   Vitamin A: 193.6 IU
                           Vitamin C: 12.7 mg.

Twenty

Desserts

APPLESAUCE

Applesauce is usually made with sugar. I think the fruit is sweet enough without it.

    4 apples, halved, cored, pitted, and finely chopped
    ½ cup water
    1 teaspoon cinnamon
    ½ teaspoon nutmeg

Mix the apples, water, and spices in a saucepan, cover, and simmer over low heat for 30 minutes, until the apples are very soft. Put the apples through a food mill. (If you don't have a food mill, you can either use a food processor or mash the apples with a fork if you like chunky applesauce. In either case, you'll have to peel the apples before cooking.) *Makes about 3 cups.*

Per ½ cup:
Calories: 71.6
Protein: 0.3 g.
Fat: 0.4 g.
Carbohydrates: 18.7 g.
Calcium: 7.6 mg.
Iron: 0.4 mg.
Sodium: 1.3 mg.
Potassium: 143 mg.
Vitamin A: 53.3 IU
Vitamin C: 2.7 mg.

CANTALOUPE WITH STRAWBERRY-MINT SAUCE

    1 cantaloupe
    ½ pint strawberries
    3 tablespoons chopped fresh mint
    2 tablespoons Grand Marnier

In a blender or food processor, purée the strawberries with the mint and Grand Marnier. Chill until ready to use.

Scoop out the cantaloupe into balls. Divide them into 4 glass bowls and top with the strawberry sauce. *Serves 4.*

Calories: 74.4   Calcium: 39.8 mg.
Protein: 1.6 g.   Iron: 1.3 mg.
Fat: 0.4 g.   Sodium: 22.3 mg.
Carbohydrates: 16.6 g.   Potassium: 308.7 mg.
                         Vitamin A: 6,096.6 IU
                         Vitamin C: 85.4 mg.

SPICED BAKED APPLES

Baked apples make a light, easy dessert and are high in fiber.

> 4 Granny Smith apples
> Lemon juice
> 2 teaspoons brown sugar
> 1 teaspoon cinnamon
> ½ teaspoon nutmeg or allspice
> ⅛ cup raisins

Slice off the top of each apple and, using a corer, remove the core without cutting through to the bottom. If the apples won't stand on their own, cut a small slice across the bottom to make them level. Sprinkle the insides with lemon juice.

Preheat the oven to 350°F.

Mix the sugar, spices, and raisins, and spoon the mixture evenly into the apples. Fill a cake or brownie pan with ¼ inch water. Place the apples in the pan, cover with aluminum foil, and bake for 30 minutes, until the apples are tender. *Serves 4.*

Calories: 127.6	Calcium: 15.9 mg.
Protein: 0.5 g.	Iron: 0.8 mg.
Fat: 0.6 g.	Sodium: 3.7 mg.
Carbohydrates: 33.4 g.	Potassium: 251.7 mg.
	Vitamin A: 80.7 IU
	Vitamin C: 4 mg.

LEMON MOUSSE

Make this mousse the same day you want to serve it; otherwise it will separate. I serve this with Raspberry Sauce (page 231), but it can easily stand on its own.

½ cup sugar
2 egg yolks
 Juice of 2 large lemons
2 tablespoons lemon rind
1 envelope gelatin
4 egg whites
1 cup low-fat yogurt

In the top of a double boiler, beat the egg yolks and sugar until pale. Whisk in the lemon juice and cook over simmering water, stirring constantly, until the mixture just begins to thicken. Remove the top from the hot water, and stir in the lemon rind and gelatin, mixing well so there are no lumps. Let the mixture sit until cool. If it gets lumpy, stir it vigorously.

Beat the egg whites until stiff. Gently fold into the lemon sauce. Then fold in the yogurt until it is just blended. Scrape the mousse into a glass bowl or individual dessert dishes, and chill at least 3 hours. *Serves 6.*

Calories: 120.4   Calcium: 56.2 mg.
Protein: 6.4 g.   Iron: 0.4 mg.
Fat: 2.6 g.   Sodium: 59.2 mg.
Carbohydrates: 16.8 g. Potassium: 117.3 mg.
                    Vitamin A: 226.1 IU
                    Vitamin C: 8 mg.

ORANGE CUPS

6 firm, large oranges
2 egg yolks
1 tablespoon sugar
2 tablespoons Grand Marnier
3 egg whites
½ cup low-fat yogurt
6 fresh mint sprigs for garnish

Cut the tops off the oranges, leaving about three-quarters of the fruit. Using a juicer, or carefully by hand, squeeze the juice from the oranges and reserve. Then, with a grapefruit knife or a spoon, scrape out the remaining white membrane so that you have 6 orange shells. Reserve.

In the top of a double boiler, beat the egg yolks with the sugar until pale, then whisk in the reserved orange juice and Grand Marnier. Cook the mixture over simmering water until it begins to foam and thicken. Remove the pan from the heat and cool.

Beat the egg whites until stiff, and fold into the orange mixture. Then fold in the yogurt until it is just blended. Divide the mousse among the orange shells, garnish with a mint sprig, and chill for at least 3 hours before serving. *Serves 6.*

Calories: 108.6   Calcium: 44.3 mg.
Protein: 4.4 g.   Iron: 0.6 mg.
Fat: 2.5 g.   Sodium: 40.7 mg.
Carbohydrates: 15.2 g.   Potassium: 227.5 mg.
                         Vitamin A: 429.7 IU
                         Vitamin C: 54.6 mg.

STRAWBERRY BAVARIAN

Bavarians, the French molded desserts, are typically made with a custard sauce, egg whites, and whipped cream. Here is a lighter version of strawberry Bavarian that makes for a very airy dessert. Serve it within 6 hours of preparing it or it will separate.

1 pint strawberries
2 tablespoons Grand Marnier
3 egg yolks
⅓ cup sugar
5 egg whites
½ cup low-fat yogurt

Purée the strawberries in a blender or food processor with the Grand Marnier. Reserve.

In the top of a double boiler, beat the egg yolks with the sugar until they are pale yellow. Stir in the puréed strawberries and cook over simmering water until the mixture begins to thicken, about 5 minutes. Remove the top of the double boiler and cool in the refrigerator.

Beat the egg whites until very stiff. Gently fold into the strawberry mixture until well blended. Fold in the yogurt until smooth. Scrape the mixture into a glass serving bowl or individual dishes, cover with plastic wrap. Chill until set, about 3 to 4 hours. *Serves 8.*

Calories: 90
Protein: 4.3 g.
Fat: 2.7 g.
Carbohydrates: 12.1 g.
Calcium: 36.6 mg.
Iron: 0.9 mg.
Sodium: 45 mg.
Potassium: 127.4 mg.
Vitamin A: 255.6 IU
Vitamin C: 24.2 mg.

APPLE SOUFFLÉ

This dessert must be served immediately, but you can make the apple-custard mixture beforehand, then add the egg whites at the last minute.

4 apples
¼ cup water
1 teaspoon allspice
2 egg yolks
2 tablespoons sugar
1 tablespoon flour
½ cup hot skim milk
1 teaspoon vanilla
4 egg whites

Peel and core the apples and cut into small pieces. Mix the apples in a saucepan with the water and simmer, covered, until tender, about 20 minutes. Stir in the allspice and purée in a food processor or blender. Reserve.

Lightly oil a soufflé dish. Preheat the oven to 375°F.

Beat the egg yolks with the sugar, then beat in the flour. Pour in the milk, whisking constantly. Transfer the mixture to a saucepan and cook, over a low heat, for 2 minutes or until the custard thickens. Stir in the vanilla, then scrape the custard into a bowl. Mix in the apples.

Beat the egg whites until stiff. Fold into the apple-custard mixture, then scrape the soufflé into the soufflé dish. Bake for 20 to 25 minutes, until the soufflé begins to brown on top. Serve immediately. *Serves 6.*

Calories: 121.7
Protein: 4.8 g.
Fat: 2.5 g.
Carbohydrates: 21.9 g.

Calcium: 38.5 mg.
Iron: 0.9 mg.
Sodium: 49.8 mg.
Potassium: 209.8 mg.
Vitamin A: 250 IU
Vitamin C: 2.8 mg.

TOFU PIE

This is a variation of my mother's cheesecake, which calls for cream cheese, egg yolks, and heavy cream. I've tried the same recipe using tofu, and the results are surprisingly good.

GRAHAM-CRACKER CRUST:
1½ cups graham-cracker crumbs
¼ cup water

TOFU FILLING:
4 (8-ounce) cakes tofu
½ cup sugar
2 teaspoons vanilla
1 teaspoon almond extract
4 egg whites

To make the crust: Mix the graham-cracker crumbs with the water, stirring until the crumbs are evenly wet. Pat the crust into the bottom and up the sides of a 10-inch spring-form pan. Set aside while you make the filling.

Preheat the oven to 350°F.

Beat the tofu with the sugar, vanilla, and almond extract until smooth, either in the blender or with a beater. Beat the egg whites in another bowl until stiff. Gently fold the tofu mixture into the egg whites. Scrape the filling into the pie crust, smoothing the top with a spatula. Bake the pie for 35 to 40 minutes, until the top begins to brown. Remove the pie from the oven and chill for several hours before serving. *Serves 12.*

Calories: 131.4	Calcium: 102.2 mg.
Protein: 6.9 g.	Iron: 1.6 mg.
Fat: 4.4 g.	Sodium: 94.7 mg.
Carbohydrates: 34.4 g.	Potassium: 83.1 mg.
	Vitamin A: 0
	Vitamin C: 0

GINGER-ALMOND TORTE

Here is a very delicate version of gingerbread that resembles an angel-food spice cake. Serve it with applesauce or fill the center with cut-up fresh fruit.

    1½ ounces almonds
     2 teaspoons ginger
     1 teaspoon cinnamon
    ½ teaspoon allspice
    ¼ teaspoon cloves
    ⅓ cup brown sugar
     2 egg yolks
     1 tablespoon granulated sugar
     5 egg whites

Preheat the oven to 350°F. Lightly oil a Bundt pan and line the bottom with waxed paper.

In a food processor or blender, finely grind the almonds. Add the spices and brown sugar and blend quickly. Reserve.

Beat the egg yolks with the granulated sugar until they are light and pale yellow, about 10 minutes. Gently fold into the almond-spice mixture.

Beat the egg whites, until very stiff, in another bowl. Then gently fold the egg whites into the almond mixture until just blended, being careful not to deflate the egg whites. Scrape the mixture evenly into the pan and bake for 30 minutes. Let the cake cool 10 minutes, then invert the pan carefully onto a plate. Run a knife around the edges to loosen and, gently, remove the pan and the waxed paper. Let the cake cool. Cut with a very sharp knife. *Serves 8.*

Calories: 117.3
Protein: 5.2 g.
Fat: 7.2 g.
Carbohydrates: 8.9 g.

Calcium: 37.2 mg.
Iron: 0.9 mg.
Sodium: 39.1 mg.
Potassium: 136.2 mg.
Vitamin A: 147.5 IU
Vitamin C: 0

COUSCOUS PUDDING

Couscous makes a surprisingly good complement to fruit. Here is a pudding served with a sauce of stewed peaches and blueberries.

1½ peaches, peeled, pitted, and chopped
 1 pint blueberries
 ½ cup couscous
1½ cups apple juice
1½ teaspoons vanilla
 1 ounce walnuts, chopped

In a saucepan, mix the peaches and blueberries with 2 table-spoons water. Cover and let the fruit steam over low heat, stirring frequently, until very soft and juicy, about 20 minutes. Remove from the heat and reserve.

In another saucepan, mix the couscous with the apple juice. Bring the liquid to a boil, then lower the heat and simmer, stirring to break up the lumps, until all the liquid is absorbed, about 7 minutes. Stir in the vanilla and walnuts.

Pour the fruit into a casserole, then spread the couscous on top. Cover and chill until set, about 2 hours. Spoon the pudding into bowls so that the fruit covers the couscous. *Serves 6.*

Calories: 118.9   Calcium: 21.2 mg.
Protein: 4.3 g.   Iron: 1.2 mg.
Fat: 3.3 g.   Sodium: 1.5 mg.
Carbohydrates: 22.4 g. Potassium: 211.2 mg.
                         Vitamin A: 579 IU
                         Vitamin C: 11.1 mg.

BROWN RICE PUDDING

½ cup cooked brown rice
2½ cups skim milk
1 teaspoon grated lemon rind
½ teaspoon nutmeg
⅛ teaspoon cloves
1 egg yolk
1 teaspoon vanilla
1½ tablespoons brown sugar
½ cup raisins
2 egg whites

Preheat the oven to 300°F.

In a saucepan, mix the rice, milk, lemon rind, and spices. Bring the milk to a simmer and cook, stirring a few times, for 10 minutes. Remove the pan from the heat and stir in the egg yolk, vanilla, brown sugar, and raisins.

Beat the egg whites until stiff, and gently stir into the brown-rice mixture. Pour the pudding into a casserole and bake for about 2 hours, until the pudding is set and brown on top. Serve or cold. *Serves 4.*

Calories: 168.4   Calcium: 175.6 mg.
Protein: 8.3 g.   Iron: 1.1 mg.
Fat: 2.8 g.   Sodium: 101 mg.
Carbohydrates: 30.7 g. Potassium: 556.7 mg.
                         Vitamin A: 150.5 IU
                         Vitamin C: 1.4 mg.

PEACH COBBLER

You can also use applesauce as a filling for this cobbler.

FILLING:
 4 peaches (about 1⅓ pounds)
½ cup brown sugar
½ cup apple juice
½ teaspoon allspice
¼ teaspoon cloves
½ teaspoon cinnamon
 1 teaspoon crystallized ginger, finely chopped

TOPPING:
⅔ cup oatmeal
⅓ cup whole-wheat flour
 2 tablespoons brown sugar
 2 tablespoons corn oil
 1 tablespoon apple juice

Peel the peaches, halve them, and remove the pits. Slice them thinly. In a saucepan, mix all the filling ingredients, cover, and simmer over low heat until the peaches are tender, about 10 minutes.
Preheat the oven to 350° F.
Mix the topping ingredients in a bowl. Spoon the filling into a baking dish, cover with the topping, and bake, covered with foil, for 20 minutes. Let sit a few minutes before serving. *Serves 4.*

Calories: 296.2   Calcium: 43.2 mg.
Protein: 3.9 g.   Iron: 2.5 mg.
Fat: 8 g.   Sodium: 2.8 mg.
Carbohydrates: 55.2 g. Potassium: 449.3 mg.
                       Vitamin A: 1,750.0 IU
                       Vitamin C: 9.9 mg.

PECAN MERINGUE COOKIES

2 egg whites
¾ cup finely chopped pecans
½ cup brown sugar

Preheat oven to 350° F.

Beat the egg whites until very stiff in a bowl. Gently fold in the pecans and brown sugar.

Drop the meringues onto a cookie sheet in 2-inch rounds. Bake for 13 to 15 minutes, until lightly browned. Remove the cookies and let them cool on racks. *Makes about 20 cookies.*

Per cookie:
Calories: 47.8
Protein: 0.8 g.
Fat: 3.2 g.
Carbohydrates: 4.5 g.

Calcium: 7 mg.
Iron: 0.3 mg.
Sodium: 7 mg.
Potassium: 46.5 mg.
Vitamin A: 5.8 IU
Vitamin C: 0.1 mg.

Index of Recipes

SOUPS

SALADS

VEGETABLES

SAUCES AND DRESSINGS

DESSERTS

Index

grilled butterflied leg of lamb,
172
guacamole, 101

Halberg, Franz, 59
heart attacks, 8, 39, 40
heart disease, 7, 31, 35, 39–45, 58, 80
 calcium and, 43
 cholesterol and, 39–41
 diet and, 40–41
 other risk factors in, 43–45
herb(s):
 spinach lasagna, 188–89
 tomato sauce, 185
 vinaigrette, 225
 see also basil; dill; mint
heredity, heart disease and, 40, 43–
 44
high-density lipoprotein (HDL),
 39–40, 45
hormones, 3, 31–32, 53, 62, 65
 in menstrual cycle, 55–59
horseradish sauce, 177–78
hypertension (high blood pressure),
 7, 8, 29, 31, 44–45
hypoglycemia, 29, 61, 64–66, 69
hypothalamus, 55, 65

Indian dishes:
 spicy chicken, 153
 sweet rice, 190
insulin, 32, 61, 62, 64, 65, 66
intestinal disorders, 35, 36

kale, 192
kebabs, vegetable, 203
kidney beans:
 enchiladas filled with, 200
 in vegetarian chili, 210
kidneys, 4, 21, 31, 32, 62

lamb:
 chops, with basil sauce, 167
 couscous, 154–55
 leg of, grilled butterflied, 172

leg of, lemon-roasted, 173
 meatballs, gingered, 174
 navarin of, 175–76
lasagna, herbed spinach, 188–89
lead, 23–24
leek(s), 91
 cucumber soup, cold, 97
legumes, 2, 9, 34
 bulgur with chick-peas, 195
 see also kidney beans; lentils
lemon:
 anchovy dressing, 99
 chicken with basil and oregano,
  142
 dill-broiled fish fillets, 124
 mousse, 235
 mustard dressing, 226
 roasted leg of lamb, 173
lentil(s), 94
 salad, 108
 soup, 94
 and vegetable stew, 197
liver, 4, 21, 29, 39, 40
low-density lipoprotein (LDL), 39–40,
 43
luteinizing hormone (LH), 55, 56–57

magnesium, 26–28
marinades:
 for lamb, 172
 for vegetables, 203
marinara sauce, 218
mayonnaise, 113
 tofu, 227
meat, 3, 4, 9
 -balls, gingered lamb, 174
 dietary guidelines for, 9
 loaf with spinach and mozzarella,
  179–80
 see also beef; lamb; veal
men, cyclical hormonal surges in, 59
menopause, 39, 40, 58, 72–73, 75–76
menorrhagia, 18
menstrual cycle, 3, 18, 30, 31, 55–59
 food cravings and, 68–69

menstrual cycle (*cont.*)
  menopause and, 39, 40, 58, 72–73,
    75–76
  see also premenstrual syndrome
meringue cookies, pecan, 244
Mexican potatoes, 215
millet, 199, 213
  with carrots, zucchini, and mint,
    198
  green peppers stuffed with, 213
mint:
  millet with carrots, zucchini and,
    198
  orange sauce, 132
  strawberry sauce, 233
  vegetable sauce, 220
Morton, Joseph, 69
mousse:
  lemon, 235
  orange, 236
mozzarella, meat loaf with spinach
  and, 179–80
muscles, 3, 29
mushroom(s), 208
  chicken with herbs and, 146
  poached sole with tomatoes and,
    130
  quail stuffed with wild rice and,
    156–57
  sauce duxelle, 163–64
  in spinach soufflé roll with vege-
    table sauce, 114–15
  veal with artichokes and, 160–61
  zucchini stuffed with brown rice
    and, 208
mussels, steamed, 138
mustard:
  lemon dressing, 226
  sauce, 162

National Academy of Sciences, 17, 46,
  47, 51
National Institutes of Health, 6–7
navarin of lamb, 176–77
nicotine, 62, 65

night blindness, 18
nitrosamines, 51
nut:
  brown rice, and fruit dressing,
    158–59
  parsley sauce, 191

obesity, 6–7, 36, 44, 53, 65, 67, 68
oils, 3, 40, 83
oilive oil, 40
omelettes:
  eggplant, 121
  tomato, onion, and basil, 119
  zucchini–red pepper, 120
onion:
  carrots with parsley and, 201
  red, salad of tomato, cucumber,
    basil and, 98
  soup, 93
  tomato, and basil omelette, 119
orange:
  chicken, 150
  cups, 236
  mint sauce, 132
  sauce, 134
  tofu dressing, 113
Oriental salad, 102
osteoporosis, 4, 24, 73–76, 58
  estrogen supplements and, 75–76
  exercise and, 76, 80
  periodontal disease and, 74–75
  symptoms of, 73–74
overweight, 45, 61, 77
  health risks of, 6–7
  obesity and, 6–7, 36, 44, 53, 65, 67,
    68
ovulation, 56, 72

parsley:
  carrots with onion and, 201
  nut sauce, 191
pasta:
  with broccoli sauce, 187
  herbed spinach lasagna, 188–89
  with herbed tomato sauce, 185

tomato(es) (*cont.*)
    veal rolls with zucchini and, 165–66
    in vegetarian chili, 210
tomato sauces:
    basic, 217
    herbed, 185
    marinara, 218
torte, ginger-almond, 240
tossed greens with anchovy-lemon
        dressing, 99
trout with orange sauce, 134
tuna and pasta salad with herbs, 110
turkey:
    mushroom and wild rice-stuffed,
        156–57
    roast, with brown rice, nut, and
        fruit dressing, 158–59

veal:
    with artichokes and mushrooms,
        160–61
    blanquette de veau, 170–71
    chops with basil sauce, 167
    with mustard sauce, 162
    roast, stuffed, 168–69
    rolls with tomatoes and zucchini,
        165–66
    scallopini with sauce duxelle,
        163–64
    stock, 222–23
vegetable(s), 2, 3, 11, 34, 43, 46, 47
    broccoli and cauliflower bowl, 202
    brown rice and, 192–93
    burnished, sauce, 165–66
    carrots with cardamom, 204
    carrots with onion and parsley,
        201
    couscous-stuffed tomatoes, 209
    dill new potatoes, 214
    eggplant Parmesan, 211
    fish fillets with, 125
    kebabs, 203
    and lentil stew, 197
    Mexican potatoes, 215
    millet-stuffed green peppers, 213

minted sauce, 220
protein in, 4
ratatouille, 207
spiced squash, 212
stuffed zucchini, 208
summer casserole, 206
and wild rice salad, 111–12
winter, soup, 95
zucchini and red peppers, 120
vegetarian chili, 212
vegetarian couscous, 197
vinaigrette:
    herb, 225
    simple, 224
vitamin A (retinol), 3, 17–18
    cancer and, 18, 46–50
    sources of, 18, 48–50, 52
    types of, 46
vitamin B complex, 18–19, 21, 31
vitamin B$_6$ (pyridoxine), 19–21
vitamin C (ascorbic acid), 21–22
    cancer and, 50–52
    sources of, 51–52
vitamin D, 3, 25, 28, 73, 75
vitamin E, 3
vitamin K, 3

walnuts, pasta with squash, tomatoes
        and, 184
watercress, 88
    beet, and endive salad, 100
    cream of, soup, 88
weight, desirable, for women, 7
weight control and weight loss, 6–8
    caloric intake and, 2, 8
    carbohydrate intake and, 35
    exercise in, 77–80
    reasons for, 6–7
wild rice, 111, 156
    and mushroom-stuffed quail,
        156–57
    and shrimp salad, 109
    and vegetable salad, 111–12
winter casserole, 199
winter vegetable soup, 95

yogurt:
    blue cheese dressing, 229
    curry dressing, 228

zinc, 30–31
zucchini:
    millet with carrots, mint and,
        198

pasta with carrots, basil and, 183
in ratatouille, 209
red pepper omelette, 120
stuffed, 208
in summer casserole, 206
veal rolls with tomatoes and,
    165–66
in vegetarian chili, 210